THE
VOCAB VIDEOS
WORKBOOK

ISBN: 978-0-615-45174-9

A-List Services LLC
50 E 42nd St, Suite 405
New York, NY 10017
(646) 216-9187
www.alisteducation.com
www.vocabvideos.com

TABLE OF CONTENTS

INTRODUCTION TO VOCAB VIDEOS

Vocabulary is a crucial part of every student's education.

It isn't one of those chores that you get in school but you'll never need in real life. Vocabulary is important because these words are actually part of the English language. You speak English. You will use English throughout *your entire life.* In high school, in college, in just about any job you get, you will use English. If you want to use English effectively, you've got to know the words.

For high school students, vocabulary is particularly important for the SAT. The correlation is simple: the more words you know, the better your Reading score on the SAT will be. Often, the only thing that makes a Reading question difficult is its vocabulary. Compare these two questions:

➤ **Dave was in a ------- mood; he was smiling and cheerful all day long.**

    (A) happy
    (B) timid
    (C) deadly
    (D) gloomy
    (E) puzzling

➤ **Dave was in a ------- mood; he was smiling and cheerful all day long.**

    (A) sanguine   *(happy)*
    (B) diffident   *(timid)*
    (C) pernicious   *(deadly)*
    (D) melancholy   *(gloomy)*
    (E) enigmatic   *(puzzling)*

Neither question is hard—*if you know what the words mean!*

Because vocabulary is so important to so many questions, we at Vocab Videos have developed a foolproof rule to help you turn the hardest Reading questions into the easiest questions:

LEARN MORE WORDS

That is all.

Luckily, we've got a great way to do that: **VOCAB VIDEOS.**

The 500 words presented in Vocab Videos were selected based on a study to determine which words occur most frequently on the SAT. This isn't just a list of words we like or some vocab trivia game where we pull out the hardest words we can find. We only chose words that have appeared frequently on the SAT.

Of course, these words appear frequently on the SAT because they're important words in the English language. So even if you're not studying for the SAT, these are important words to know.

So, how do you get started?

1. Watch the videos

Go to **www.vocabvideos.com** and log into your account. (Or, if you don't have an account, create one!)

You should watch at least an entire 5-word chapter every time you go to the site. You should plan on watching at least 5 words a day, 4 days a week. That will get you through one 20-word episode a week. If you want to go faster, you can try 10 words a day, getting you through 2 episodes a week. Find the pace that's right for you.

2. Absorb the Words

You won't remember the word perfectly after the first time you watch a video. You'll need help.

On the website there are worksheets that allow you to take notes to help you remember. You can either print them out or save your notes online to access anytime. At the end of each video, the word and its definition will appear on the screen. Quickly pause the video and write the definition of the word on those worksheets. Or you can take notes in this workbook.

Think of your brain as a sponge and the vocabulary words you just catalogued as water. You need to soak it up— every drop! You may be thinking, "But, how?" Everyone is different.

- Sometimes a student can absorb a word after just one viewing (rare).
- Some need multiple viewings (not rare).
- Some need to write the word, its definition, and craft a sentence using the word (recommended).
- Some need to read their worksheets over and over again (by *some*, we mean *most*).
- Some turn their notes into flashcards. The site has a built-in multimedia flashcard maker to help (great!)
- Some try using their newfound words with their friends.

> "Oh my god, that song is so hackneyed."
> "Dude, why are so diffident? Ask her out!"

- Some use mnemonic devices. Mnemonic devices are memory tricks you can play to help connect a word and its meaning in your head. People remember things more easily when they have **concrete pictures** to go with them.

> *Undermine* means to "weaken". Imagine: if you dig a <u>mine</u> <u>under</u> a house, you will weaken the foundation.

> *Sagacious* means "wise". Imagine a very wise, very old monk, living on the top of a tall mountain. He is so old that his skin is beginning to <u>sag</u> off of his face.

> Stupid? Perhaps. But the more memorable you make them, the easier they'll be to recall. It's always the really annoying jingles that get stuck in your head for days.

- **SOME DO ALL OF THE ABOVE.**

Think you have truly absorbed all of the words for a particular episode? Then, test yourself with the quiz that is provided at the end of each episode. If you get a question wrong, it makes sense to review that particular word again. In fact, even if you get every question right, you should still review all of the words from time to time.

3. Review

Let's be realistic: you're going to forget some of the words. For example, what does *pernicious* mean? What about *sanguine*? We just told you on the first page. You forgot, didn't you? DIDN'T YOU? That's why you have to review. In fact, we insist. After every 100 words (or 5 episodes), stop and check over your worksheets and take the quizzes again.

You may be thinking, "And, what if I fail the quizzes?"

Watch the videos *again*!
Absorb the words *again*!
Review *again*!

That's why we have this book. It lists all 500 words from all 500 videos with tons of information to help you review. The words are grouped by episodes with a list at the beginning showing the words and definitions in that episode.

On the left side of each page you'll find:

- ✒ The **word** itself.
- ✒ The word's **part of speech** (noun, verb, or adjective).
- ✒ An easy-to-read **pronunciation guide**.
- ✒ Some **blank lines** for you to write definitions, sentences, mnemonic devices, or anything you want to help remember the words.

On the right you'll find:

- ✒ The **definition** of the word. Note that sometimes a word may have two different but related definitions.
- ✒ The **example sentence** used in the original video.

Some, but not all, words may also have:

- ✒ **Synonyms**: A list of other words that have the same meaning as this word
- ✒ **Categories**: Sometimes, words have similar or overlapping meanings. We've grouped these into categories with names to help you associate these words with each other. Note that members of a given category may not be *exact* synonyms, but simply have related meanings. See *Appendix C* in this book for a list of all the categories and the words they contain.
- ✒ **Word Alerts**: These notes give additional forms of the word, either by changing its part of speech or by adding prefixes or suffixes. They also give information about roots and relationships between words.

Here's an example of a word and all its information:

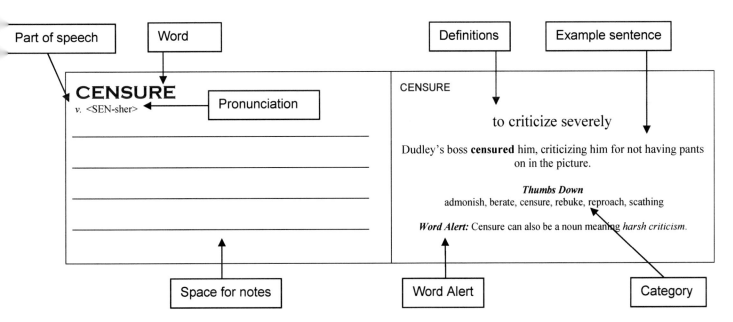

You can also use this book to **quiz yourself.** Fold the page in half along the middle line so you only see the left side, keeping the right side hidden. Try to remember the definitions of all the words without looking at the right side. Quiz yourself on all the words in the episode before moving on to the next one.

This book also has some Appendices at the back for your reference.

- **Appendix A** lists all the words in alphabetical order and the episodes they appear in.
- **Appendix B** lists all the episodes in the order they appear on the website and the words they contain.
- **Appendix C** lists all the categories shown on the cards, the words in each category, and their definitions.

All these things are tools you can use **to help you remember these words**. Remember: it's not enough to learn the words just so you'll pass the quiz. The point is to remember them *forever:* when you take the SAT, or any time you encounter them as you go through college and beyond.

- **I was in a ------- mood upon discovering that I had scored an 800 on the SAT Reading. (Thanks Vocab Videos!)**

  (A) sanguine
  (B) diffident
  (C) pernicious
  (D) melancholy
  (E) enigmatic

Two's Company Part 1

Hank and Dudley are colleagues with very different approaches to work and how to win over the new girl in the office.

INUNDATE	to overwhelm with; to flood
GARISH	flashy, tastelessly loud and brightly colored
UNDERSCORE	to emphasize
HAUGHTY	snobbish; overly proud
TRANSIENT	existing only briefly
URBANE	polite, suave, and cultivated in manner
METICULOUS	extremely careful
DISSEMINATE	to spread out
CENSURE	to criticize severely
SURREPTITIOUS	done or made by secret or stealthy means
MELANCHOLY	sad; gloomy
ASPIRE	to have a great ambition
CONCORD	agreement
DILIGENT	hard working
REPREHENSIBLE	deserving of criticism or disapproval
EXALT	to elevate, glorify, or praise
FLAMBOYANT	highly elaborate; showy
ASSESS	to make a judgment about
SAGACIOUS	insightful and wise
PARADOX	a seemingly contradictory statement that may nonetheless be true

INUNDATE
v. <in-UHN-dayt>

_____
_____
_____
_____

GARISH
adj. <GAIR-ish>

_____
_____
_____
_____

UNDERSCORE
v. <UN-der-skohr>

_____
_____
_____
_____

HAUGHTY
adj. <HAW-tee>

_____
_____
_____
_____

TRANSIENT
adj. <TRAN-zee-uhnt>

_____
_____
_____
_____
_____

INUNDATE

to overwhelm with; to flood

Dudley was **inundated** with Hank's folders; his desk was flooded with paperwork.

GARISH

flashy, tastelessly loud and brightly colored

Dudley's tie was **garish**; it was offensively tasteless.

Flashy
flamboyant, florid, garish, ornate

UNDERSCORE

to emphasize

Hank **underscored** his feelings for Nina, emphasizing how attractive he thinks she is.

HAUGHTY

snobbish; overly proud

Hank was **haughty**, arrogantly acting like he knows more about fashion than Dudley.

Cocky
bombastic, condescend, grandiose, haughty, patronize, pompous, pretentious

TRANSIENT

existing only briefly

Dudley's confidence was **transient**; it lasted for only a few seconds.

Gone with the Wind
elusive, ephemeral, evanescent, evasive, transient, transitory

URANE
adj. <ur-BANE>

_____

_____

_____

_____

URBANE

polite, suave, and cultivated in manner

While Nina is truly **urbane** and knows a lot about classical music, Hank is just pretending.

METICULOUS
adj. <muh-TIK-yoo-luhs>

_____

_____

_____

_____

METICULOUS

extremely careful

Dudley was **meticulous** about his appearance, paying attention to every detail.

Synonyms: conscientious, scrupulous

DISSEMINATE
v. <di-SEM-uh-nayt>

_____

_____

_____

_____

DISSEMINATE

to spread out

Hank **disseminated** the picture of Dudley, sending an email to everyone in the office.

CENSURE
v. <SEN-sher>

_____

_____

_____

_____

CENSURE

to criticize severely

Dudley's boss **censured** him, criticizing him for not having pants on in the picture.

Thumbs Down
admonish, berate, censure, rebuke, reproach, scathing

Word Alert: Censure can also be a noun meaning *harsh criticism.*

SURREPTITIOUS
adj. <sur-uhp-TISH-uhs>

_____

_____

_____

_____

SURREPTITIOUS

done or made by secret or stealthy means

Dudley **surreptitiously** announced his love for Nina, writing her a secret note while no one was looking.

Synonyms: clandestine

MELANCHOLY
adj. <MEL-uhn-kaw-lee>

_____

_____

_____

_____

MELANCHOLY

sad; gloomy

Dudley has become **melancholy**; the thought of losing his job is very depressing.

Cry Baby
despair, despondent, dour, lament, melancholy, morose

Word Alert: Melancholy can also be a noun meaning *sadness*.

ASPIRE
v. <uh-SPIRE>

_____

_____

_____

_____

ASPIRE

to have a great ambition

Hank **aspires** to move up in the company and wants to become a successful executive.

CONCORD
n. <KON-kord>

_____

_____

_____

_____

CONCORD

agreement

Hank and Dudley reached a **concord**, agreeing to work together on the project.

Like-Minded
accord, concord, concur, conform, consensus, uniform

DILIGENT
adj. <DIL-i-juhnt>

_____

_____

_____

_____

DILIGENT

hard working

Dudley worked **diligently** through the night; Hank did not.

Synonyms: assiduous

REPREHENSIBLE
adj. <rep-ri-HEN-suh-buhl>

_____

_____

_____

_____

REPREHENSIBLE

deserving of criticism or disapproval

Hank taking credit for the assignment was **reprehensible**, a terrible act deserving of blame.

EXALT
v. <eg-ZAWLT>

_____

_____

_____

_____

FLAMBOYANT
adj. <flam-BOY-uhnt>

_____

_____

_____

_____

ASSESS
v. <uh-SESS>

_____

_____

_____

_____

SAGACIOUS
adj. <suh-GAY-shuhs>

_____

_____

_____

_____

PARADOX
n. <PAIR-uh-doks>

_____

_____

_____

_____

EXALT

to elevate, glorify, or praise

The boss **exalted** Hank for his work on the assignment, praising his efforts.

Hip Hip Hooray!
acclaim, adulation, commend, exalt, extol, laud

FLAMBOYANT

highly elaborate; showy

Hank **flamboyantly** expressed his feelings for Nina, in an elaborate show of affection.

Flashy
flamboyant, florid, garish, ornate

ASSESS

to make a judgment about

Nina **assessed** Hank's character by judging his behavior around the office.

SAGACIOUS

insightful and wise

Nina made a wise decision, after considering Hank's flaws, she **sagaciously** chose to date Dudley.

Wise Guy
circumspect, discreet, judicious, prudent, sagacious, shrewd

Word Alert: A *sage* is a sagacious person. *Sagacity* is the quality of being sagacious.

PARADOX

a seemingly contradictory statement that may nonetheless be true

Dudley's final line "Sometimes nothing is everything" is a **paradox**.

Two's Company Part 2

April employs some unusual methods to try to ease the tension between her brother Hank and Dudley.

RANCOR	hostility
IMPARTIAL	not biased
SANCTION	to give official authorization or approval to
MERCENARY	motivated solely by a desire for monetary or material gain
INDUCE	to bring about the occurrence of
TRACTABLE	easily managed, led, or taught
VOLUBLE	characterized by ready and rapid speech
REITERATE	to repeat
CURTAIL	to cut short
DEBILITATE	to weaken
INFLAMMATORY	arousing strong emotion, esp. anger
EQUANIMITY	calmness
DETER	to prevent or discourage from acting
VEILED	concealed or disguised
DISCORD	lack of agreement, quarreling
INQUISITIVE	showing curiosity
DIVERGENT	drawing apart from a common point; differing from another
REPROACH	to criticize or express disappointment
REMINISCE	to recollect and tell of the past
SANGUINE	cheerful

RANCOR
n. <RANK-er>

_____

_____

_____

_____

RANCOR

hostility

When he visited his family, Hank became filled with **rancor** and screamed at his mother.

Bad Blood
abhor, acrimony, animosity, antagonistic, contempt, disdain, enmity, rancor, scorn

---

IMPARTIAL
adj. <im-PAHR-shuhl>

_____

_____

_____

_____

IMPARTIAL

not biased

April is **impartial** about Hank's fight with Dudley; she hasn't taken a side.

Synonyms: dispassionate

SANCTION
v. <SANK-shuhn>

_____

_____

_____

_____

SANCTION

to give official authorization or approval to

The Sleeping Mind Institute has **sanctioned** April by giving her a certificate authorizing her to perform hypnosis.

Word Alert: Sanction is a rare case of a word that is its own opposite: it can also mean *to punish so as to deter.* Crazy!
Word Alert: Sanction can also be a noun meaning *an authorization* or *a punishment.*

MERCENARY
adj. <MUR-suh-ner-ee>

_____

_____

_____

_____

MERCENARY

motivated solely by a desire for monetary or material gain

April has a **mercenary** motive for helping Hank; she only cares about getting paid.

Word Alert: Mercenary can also be a noun meaning *one who works or serves for mercenary reasons.*

INDUCE
v. <in-DOOS>

_____

_____

_____

_____

INDUCE

to bring about the occurrence of

April **induces** a trance in Hank, as her use of the candle makes him fall into a hypnotic state.

TRACTABLE
adj. <TRAK-tuh-buhl>

_____

_____

_____

_____

TRACTABLE

easily managed, led, or taught

During his trance, Hank is incredibly **tractable** and will do anything that April commands.

Synonyms: docile

Word Alert: If the prefix *in-* means *not*, what would *intractable* mean?

VOLUBLE
adj. <VOL-yuh-buhl>

_____

_____

_____

_____

VOLUBLE

characterized by ready and rapid speech

Hank suddenly becomes **voluble**, listing his problems quickly and extensively.

Synonyms: garrulous, verbose

REITERATE
v. <ree-IT-uh-rayt>

_____

_____

_____

_____

REITERATE

to repeat

To help him think positively, Hank and April **reiterated** a phrase over and over again.

CURTAIL
v. <ker-TAYL>

_____

_____

_____

_____

CURTAIL

to cut short

Hank and April's meditation was **curtailed** by their mother's rude interruption, and they had to stop.

DEBILITATE
v. <di-BIL-i-tayt>

_____

_____

_____

_____

DEBILITATE

to weaken

Hank imagines that Dudley is **debilitated** by a painful, painful shot to the groin.

Synonyms: enervate

INFLAMMATORY
adj. <in-FLAM-uh-tor-ee>

_____

_____

_____

_____

INFLAMMATORY

arousing strong emotion, esp. anger

Dudley's arrival was **inflammatory**, as Hank exploded in anger at the sight of him.

Synonyms: provocative

EQUANIMITY
n. <eh-qua-NIH-mih-tee>

_____

_____

_____

_____

EQUANIMITY

calmness

April displays **equanimity**, keeping calm while Hank and Dudley lose their cool.

Chill
composed, equanimity, placid, serene, tranquil

DETER
v. <di-TUR>

_____

_____

_____

_____

DETER

to prevent or discourage from acting

The machine is designed to **deter** Hank; it is meant to prevent him from attacking Dudley

Word Alert: A *deterrent* is something used to deter.

VEILED
adj. <VAYLD>

_____

_____

_____

_____

VEILED

concealed or disguised

Hank's comments may sound like compliments, but they are really **veiled** insults.

DISCORD
n. <DIS-kord>

_____

_____

_____

_____

DISCORD

lack of agreement, quarreling

Hank and Dudley are in **discord**; they disagree about whether Dudley stole Nina or not.

Word Alert: Something *discordant* is full of discord.

INQUISITIVE
adj. <in-KWIZ-i-tiv>

_____

_____

_____

DIVERGENT
adj. <di-VUR-juhnt>

_____

_____

_____

REPROACH
v. <ri-PROHCH>

_____

_____

_____

REMINISCE
v. <re-mi-NISS>

_____

_____

_____

SANGUINE
adj. <SAN-gwin>

_____

_____

_____

_____

INQUISITIVE

showing curiosity

Dudley is **inquisitive** about how he should draw Hank and asks April for more information.

DIVERGENT

drawing apart from a common point; differing from another

Hank and Dudley have **divergent** ideas about each other, drawing pictures that were radically different.

Word Alert: To *diverge* is to become divergent.
Word Alert: If the prefix *con-* means *together*, what would *convergent* mean?

REPROACH

to criticize or express disappointment

April **reproached** Hank for not even trying to make up with Dudley.

Thumbs Down
admonish, berate, censure, rebuke, reproach, scathing

Word Alert: Reproach can also be a noun meaning *an act of criticism or blame.*

REMINISCE

to recollect and tell of the past

Hank **reminisced** with Dudley, remembering all the times he had humiliated him over the years.

Word Alert: Reminiscence is the act of reminiscing. Something that is *reminiscent* causes reminiscence.

SANGUINE

cheerful

Hank suddenly became **sanguine** when he cheerfully realized that he likes being single.

Happy Camper
buoyant, ecstasy, elated, euphoria, felicity, mirth, sanguine

Two's Company Part 3

Hank and Dudley's client presentation takes a turn for the worse and they scramble to try and recover their dignity and the account.

NONCHALANT	casually unconcerned (sometimes falsely)
DILATORY	tending to delay; late or slow
SUPERFLUOUS	extra, unnecessary
CONDESCEND	to deal with people in a superior manner
ACRIMONY	hostility
PRODIGIOUS	enormous; extraordinary
DAUNT	to intimidate or lessen one's courage
TEDIOUS	tiresomely long or boring
MEDIOCRE	ordinary; so-so
MANDATE	an authoritative command
RESIGNATION	acceptance of something as inescapable
NURTURE	to help develop, to nourish
FERVENT	greatly emotional or enthusiastic
ECLECTIC	having elements from a variety of sources
COMPOSED	calm
VERSATILE	capable of doing many things well
SCATHING	harshly critical
ELOQUENT	well spoken
COMMEND	to praise
ECSTASY	intense joy or delight

NONCHALANT
adj. <NON-shah-LONT>

_____

_____

_____

_____

NONCHALANT

casually unconcerned (sometimes falsely)

Hank is **nonchalant** about the presentation; he's not worried at all.

Synonyms: indifferent, apathetic

DILATORY
adj. <DIL-uh-tor-ee>

_____

_____

_____

_____

DILATORY

tending to delay; late or slow

Dudley is **dilatory**; he's always late.

SUPERFLUOUS
adj. <soo-PER-floo-us>

_____

_____

_____

_____

SUPERFLUOUS

extra, unnecessary

Dudley's 7 bags are **superfluous**, he can't possibly need them all for a day trip.

Synonyms: gratuitous

CONDESCEND
v. <con-duh-SEND>

_____

_____

_____

_____

CONDESCEND

to deal with people in a superior manner

Hank is **condescending** to Dudley, he speaks down to him in a superior manner.

Cocky
bombastic, condescend, grandiose, haughty, patronize, pompous, pretentious

---

ACRIMONY
n. <AK-rih-moh-nee>

_____

_____

_____

_____

ACRIMONY

hostility

There is **acrimony** between Hank and Dudley; Hank is incredibly hostile towards his colleague.

Bad Blood
abhor, acrimony, animosity, antagonistic, contempt, disdain, enmity, rancor, scorn

PRODIGIOUS
adj. <pruh-DIH-juhs>

_____

_____

_____

PRODIGIOUS

enormous; extraordinary

The building where Dudley and Hank must deliver their presentation is **prodigious** in its extraordinary size.

Synonyms: copious, voluminous

DAUNT
v. <DAWNT>

_____

_____

_____

DAUNT

to intimidate or lessen one's courage

Hank and Dudley are **daunted** by Mr. Smallwood, his tremendous size was very intimidating.

Word Alert: Someone who is *undaunted* is not afraid.

TEDIOUS
adj. <TEE-dee-uhs>

_____

_____

_____

TEDIOUS

tiresomely long or boring

Hank and Dudley's presentation was **tedious**; it was so long and boring that it caused Mr. Smallwood to fall asleep.

Word Alert: Tedium is the quality of being tedious.

MEDIOCRE
adj. <mee-dee-OH-ker>

_____

_____

_____

_____

MEDIOCRE

ordinary; so-so

Mr. Smallood objects that every year the presentation is **mediocre**; it's just ordinary.

Word Alert: Mediocrity is the state or quality of being mediocre.

MANDATE
n. <MAN-dayt>

_____

_____

_____

_____

MANDATE

an authoritative command

Mr. Smallwood issued a **mandate** to Hank and Dudley, giving them an authoritative command to revise their presentation.

Word Alert: A *mandate* is something that is mandatory.

RESIGNATION
n. <re-zig-NAY-shun>

_____

_____

_____

_____

RESIGNATION

acceptance of something as inescapable

Hank had a feeling of **resignation**, believing that there was nothing he could do to fix the presentation.

Word Alert: To be *resigned* is to feel resignation.

NURTURE
v. <NUR-cher>

_____

_____

_____

_____

NURTURE

to help develop, to nourish

Dudley **nurtured** Hank, offering kind words and support to get him back to his old self.

Synonyms: foster

FERVENT
adj. <FUR-vuhnt>

_____

_____

_____

_____

FERVENT

greatly emotional or enthusiastic

Hank becomes **fervent** as he enthusiastically regains his confidence.

X-treme Intensity!
ardor, fervent, galvanize, impassioned, zealous

Word Alert: *Fervor* is a fervent feeling.

ECLECTIC
adj. <e-KLEK-tik>

_____

_____

_____

_____

ECLECTIC

having elements from a variety of sources

The contents of Dudley's luggage are **eclectic**, there are all different kinds of items.

COMPOSED
adj. <kuhm-POHZD>

_____

_____

_____

_____

COMPOSED

calm

Hank and Dudley are **composed**, calm and ready for the presentation.

Chill
composed, equanimity, placid, serene, tranquil

Word Alert: *Composure* is the state of being composed.
Word Alert: Composed also means *made up of.*

VERSATILE
adj. <VUR-suh-tahyl>

_____

_____

_____

_____

SCATHING
adj. <SKAYTHE-ing (rhymes with *bathing*)>

_____

_____

_____

_____

ELOQUENT
adj. <EH-lo-quent>

_____

_____

_____

_____

COMMEND
v. <kuh-MEND>

_____

_____

_____

_____

ECSTASY
n. <EK-stuh-see>

_____

_____

_____

_____

_____

VERSATILE

capable of doing many things well

Hank and Dudley show that they're **versatile**; they can do many things well.

SCATHING

harshly critical

Mr. Smallwood is **scathing** about the new presentation; he is extremely harsh in his criticism.

Thumbs Down
admonish, berate, censure, rebuke, reproach, scathing

ELOQUENT

well spoken

Dudley is **eloquent** when he addresses Mr. Smallwood, he speaks well and fluently.

Synonyms: articulate

Word Alert: The -*loq*- root means *speech*, so someone *loquacious* is *talkative.*

COMMEND

to praise

Mr. Smallwood **commends** Dudley, he praises him for his speech.

Hip Hip Hooray!
acclaim, adulation, commend, exalt, extol, laud

ECSTASY

intense joy or delight

Hank and Dudley are in **ecstasy** when they hear the contract is renewed, they are absolutely delighted.

Happy Camper
buoyant, ecstasy, elated, euphoria, felicity, mirth, sanguine

Word Alert: If you are *ecstatic* you are filled with ecstasy.

TWO'S COMPANY PART 4

There's a new boss in the office and Hank must enlist Dudley's help to try to save his job.

DESPAIR	a complete loss of hope
EXONERATE	to free from blame or responsibility
JUXTAPOSE	to place side by side
EVASIVE	tending to escape
CURSORY	performed with haste and little attention to detail
DISPARAGE	to speak of in an insulting way
ELITE	superior in status
BANE	a cause of death or ruin
DEFER	to submit or yield to another's wish or opinion
AVERSE	reluctant
ENMITY	hatred
GUILE	skillful deceit
DOGMATIC	stubbornly and arrogantly opinionated
WARRANT	to justify
FRENETIC	wildly excited; frenzied; frantic
CONVOLUTED	complicated
PLAUSIBLE	believable
HAIL	to salute or greet
ENUNCIATE	to pronounce with clarity
FELICITY	great happiness

DESPAIR

n. <di-SPAIR>

Bruce Wayne was in despair after the death of his parents.

DESPAIR

a complete loss of hope

Dudley is in a state of **despair** because his cat's death left him feeling sad and hopeless.

Cry Baby
despair, despondent, dour, lament, melancholy, morose

Word Alert: Despair can also be a verb meaning *to lose hope.*

EXONERATE

v. <eg-ZON-uh-rayt>

At paintball locations, they make you sign waivers to exornate themselves from any injuries

EXONERATE

to free from blame or responsibility

Hank's research **exonerated** Dudley; he was not to blame for Jeepers' death.

Synonyms: vindicate

JUXTAPOSE

v. <JUHK-stuh-pohz>

James juxtaposed the two boys side by side for their picture together.

JUXTAPOSE

to place side by side

Dudley **juxtaposed** the two pictures, holding a picture of the skinny Jeepers next to the fat Jeepers.

EVASIVE

adj. <ih-VAY-siv>

The evasive nature of the thief made him very difficult to catch.

EVASIVE

tending to escape

Dudley used **evasive** maneuvers to escape from Hank as they ran through the office.

Gone with the Wind
elusive, ephemeral, evanescent, evasive, transient, transitory

Word Alert: To *evade* means to escape.
Word Alert: Evasive is also similar in meaning to *equivocal.*

CURSORY

adj. <KUR-suh-ree>

The amateur artist had a very cursory fashion in his paintings, it wasn't very detailed.

CURSORY

performed with haste and little attention to detail

Hank read the files in a **cursory** fashion; he quickly glanced at the titles but paid little attention to the details.

DISPARAGE
v. <di-SPAIR-ij>

The bully disparaged the young boy for not standing up to himself.

DISPARAGE

to speak of in an insulting way

The Boss **disparaged** Hank for his poor work, calling him an idiot and saying he behaved like a child.

Trash Talk
belittle, decry, denigrate, denounce, deprecate, deride, disparage, vilify

---

ELITE
adj. <ih-LEET>

~~the new~~ *The upperclassmen of British colonial society were considered to be elite to that of the colonists.*

ELITE

superior in status

The new boss is **elite** in many ways; he went to a top school, belongs to an exclusive club and drives a luxury car.

Word Alert: An *elitist* is a person who believes he is superior (often wrongly).

BANE
n. <rhymes wih *cane*>

"Homework is the bane of my existence" said Tom.

BANE

a cause of death or ruin

To Hank, the new boss is the **bane** of his existence – the embodiment of everything that can ruin him.

Killer
bane, deleterious, pernicious

DEFER
v. <di-FUR>

Nick deferred to his sister's request to let her watch TV.

DEFER

to submit or yield to another's wish or opinion

Hank must **defer** to his new boss's request and accept that he must shine the man's shoes with his tie.

Word Alert: *Deference* is the act of deferring.

AVERSE
adj. <uh-VURS>

Rob was averse to go to school on Monday.

AVERSE

reluctant

Hank was **averse** to cleaning the bathroom; he really did not want to do it.

Word Alert: Don't confuse this word with *adverse* [see *adversity*].

ENMITY
n. <EN-mi-tee>

The enmity that Hitler had towards the Jews was despicable.

ENMITY

hatred

It was easy to see that Hank hated his new boss; the **enmity** he felt for him was obvious.

Bad Blood
abhor, acrimony, animosity, antagonistic, contempt, disdain, enmity, rancor, scorn

---

GUILE
n. <GUYL>

Using guile, the con artist tricked the boy into losing all of his money

GUILE

skillful deceit

Using **guile** to trick Hank, the man skillfully deceived him and exposed his lie.

Shady
cunning, duplicity, guile, treachery

DOGMATIC
adj. <dog-MAT-ic>

The dogmatic college professor insisted that proper use of the word "there" when it was really "their"

DOGMATIC

stubbornly and arrogantly opinionated

Dogmatic about the use of paper clips, Hank's new boss stubbornly insisted that he use paper clips instead of staples.

Pig-Headed
dogged, dogmatic, intransigent, obdurate, obstinate, tenacity

Word Alert: *Dogma* is the set of beliefs that a dogmatic person holds.

WARRANT
v. <WAR-uhnt>

"The ends warrants the means"- Maechiavelli

WARRANT

to justify

To justify his decision to fire Hank, the new boss lists a number of reasons which **warrant** Hank's dismissal.

FRENETIC
adj. <fruh-NET-ik>

The boy was frenetic when his threw him a surprise party.

FRENETIC

wildly excited; frenzied; frantic

Hank was **frenetic** when he called Dudley, frantically explaining that he is about to be fired.

THE STUDY PARTNER

April is trying to study words for the SAT and an uninvited guest would like to help.

MUNDANE	ordinary, commonplace
ENIGMATIC	puzzling
KEEN	sharp, perceptive
SKEPTICAL	doubting, questioning, not believing
ENCROACH	to advance beyond limits
JUDICIOUS	having good judgment, prudent
INACCESSIBLE	not easily approached, entered, or obtained
THERAPEUTIC	having healing powers
SPORADIC	occurring at irregular intervals
BUTTRESS	to support or strengthen
PLACID	calm, quiet
AMIABLE	friendly
PROPENSITY	tendency
PERNICIOUS	deadly or destructive
CONFOUND	to confuse
DISPEL	to rid of
SUBDUE	to bring under control
HARANGUE	a long, angry speech
EARNEST	showing deep sincerity or seriousness
INNOCUOUS	harmless

MUNDANE
adj. <muhn-DAYN>

_____

_____

_____

_____

MUNDANE

ordinary, commonplace

Spending her nights studying SAT vocabulary was **mundane** for April; it was a routine part of her weekends.

Played Out
banal, hackneyed, insipid, mundane, prosaic, trite

ENIGMATIC
adj. <en-ig-MAT-ik>

_____

_____

_____

_____

ENIGMATIC

puzzling

April couldn't grasp the **enigmatic** comments made by the mysterious caller; they were utterly puzzling.

What the—?
abstruse, ambiguous, amorphous, enigmatic, equivocal, esoteric, nebulous

Word Alert: An *enigma* is an enigmatic thing.

KEEN
adj. <KEEN>

_____

_____

_____

_____

KEEN

sharp, perceptive

The caller was so **keen** and perceptive; he could discern that April was stressed about the upcoming SAT just from listening to her voice.

Eagle Eye
acuity, astute, discern, incisive, keen, perspicacity

SKEPTICAL
adj. <SKEP-ti-kuhl>

_____

_____

_____

_____

SKEPTICAL

doubting, questioning, not believing

April was **skeptical** of the caller's motives, doubting he actually wanted to study vocabulary with her.

Synonyms: incredulous

Word Alert: A *skeptic* is a skeptical person. *Skepticism* is the state of being skeptical.

ENCROACH
v. <en-KROHCH>

_____

_____

_____

_____

_____

ENCROACH

to advance beyond limits

The unwelcome Study Partner **encroached** on April's space, frightening her as he tried to break into her house.

JUDICIOUS
adj. <joo-DISH-uhs>

_____

_____

_____

_____

JUDICIOUS

having good judgment, prudent

April's decision to watch scary movies before bed was not a **judicious** one; she didn't use her best judgment.

Wise Guy
circumspect, discreet, judicious, prudent, sagacious, shrewd

INACCESSIBLE
adj. <in-uhk-SES-uh-buhl>

_____

_____

_____

_____

INACCESSIBLE

not easily approached, entered, or obtained

Secure in her house, April was **inaccessible** to the Study Partner's advances, or so she thought…

THERAPEUTIC
adj. <thair-uh-PYOO-tik>

_____

_____

_____

_____

THERAPEUTIC

having healing powers

April hoped the sleeping pills would have a healing, **therapeutic** effect, helping to stop her bad dreams, so she could finally get some rest.

SPORADIC
adj. <spuh-RAD-ik>

_____

_____

_____

_____

SPORADIC

occurring at irregular intervals

The Study Partner continued to scare April by playing with the lights **sporadically**; he was turning them on and off at irregular intervals.

BUTTRESS
v. <BUH-tris>

_____

_____

_____

_____

BUTTRESS

to support or strengthen

April attempted to **buttress** the door, supporting it with her chair in order to keep the Study Partner out.

Synonyms: bolster

Word Alert: Buttress can also be a noun meaning *something used for support*.

PLACID

adj. <PLAS-id>

_____

_____

_____

_____

PLACID

calm, quiet

After all the disturbances, it appeared that April's room had finally become quiet and **placid**.

Chill
composed, equanimity, placid, serene, tranquil

AMIABLE

adj. <AY-mee-uh-buhl>

_____

_____

_____

_____

AMIABLE

friendly

The **amiable** pizza deliveryman was extremely friendly toward April, telling her that all of their pies "are topped with smiles."

BFF
amiable, affable, amicable, camaraderie, cordial, genial

PROPENSITY

n. <pruh-PEN-si-tee>

_____

_____

_____

_____

PROPENSITY

tendency

The friendly deliveryman had a **propensity** for forgetting things; he tended to be very absentminded.

Synonyms: predilection

PERNICIOUS

adj. <per-NISH-uhs>

_____

_____

_____

_____

PERNICIOUS

deadly or destructive

April hoped the knife will have a **pernicious**, deadly effect; she wants to get rid of the intrusive Study Partner once and for all!

Killer
bane, deleterious, pernicious

CONFOUND

v. <kon-FOUND>

_____

_____

_____

_____

CONFOUND

to confuse

Confused as to why the Study Partner won't leave her alone, April is totally **confounded** by the strange situation.

Synonyms: bemuse

DISPEL
v. <dis-SPEL>

_____

_____

_____

_____

SUBDUE
v. <sub-DOO>

_____

_____

_____

_____

HARANGUE
n. <huh-RANG>

_____

_____

_____

_____

EARNEST
adj. <ER-nest>

_____

_____

_____

_____

INNOCUOUS
adj. <in-NOK-yoo-us>

_____

_____

_____

_____

DISPEL

to rid of

April wants to **dispel** the Study Partner from her dreams—to get rid of him, so she can finally get some rest.

SUBDUE

to bring under control

Spraying his eyes, April tries to **subdue** the Study Partner to bring him under control so she no longer has to be afraid.

Synonyms: quell, suppress

HARANGUE

a long, angry speech

April **harangues** the unwanted Study Partner—even calling him a monster—in her long, angry speech.

Word Alert: Harangue can also be a verb meaning *to speak or write in an angry or violent manner.*

EARNEST

showing deep sincerity or seriousness

The Study Partner appears sincere and **earnest** when telling April he just wants to help her study SAT vocab.

Serious Business
earnest, solemn, somber

INNOCUOUS

harmless

April realizes that despite his menacing appearance, the Study Partner is **innocuous**; he is harmless after all.

RUMOR CHICK: THE DIARY

Mystic Dan must delve into Pamela's past to see if he can save her friendship with Laura.

CACOPHONY	jarring, disagreeable sound
CLAIRVOYANCE	the power to see things that cannot be perceived by the senses
INCISIVE	penetrating, clear and sharp
BENIGN	kind; beneficial
VACILLATE	to be undecided, to hesitate
OBSTREPEROUS	noisily and stubbornly defiant
BELITTLE	to speak of in an insulting way
VOLUMINOUS	big; having large volume
ARCHAIC	outdated; really old
PATRONIZE	to treat condescendingly
INCONTROVERTIBLE	impossible to dispute
PRECARIOUS	dangerously unstable or insecure
DISMISS	to reject
OBSTINATE	stubborn
DISSIPATE	to disappear
CIRCUMVENT	to avoid or get around
INDIGNATION	anger (over something unjust)
PENITENT	feeling or expressing remorse
GENIAL	friendly, cheerful
INCORRIGIBLE	incapable of being corrected or reformed

CACOPHONY

n. <kuh-KOFF-o-nee>

_____

_____

_____

_____

CACOPHONY

jarring, disagreeable sound

Mystic Dan creates a loud **cacophony** of sound to try to get people's attention.

Noise Pollution
boisterous, cacophony, obstreperous, tumultuous

Word Alert: Something *cacophonous* sounds like a cacophony.
Word Alert: If the prefix *eu-* means *good*, what would *euphony* mean?

CLAIRVOYANCE

n. <klair-VOY-unss>

_____

_____

_____

_____

CLAIRVOYANCE

the power to see things that cannot be perceived by the senses

Mystic Dan possesses **clairvoyance**: he can sees things about Pamela's future.

INCISIVE

adj. <in-SAHY-siv>

_____

_____

_____

_____

INCISIVE

penetrating, clear and sharp

Mystic Dan's sharp, **incisive** comments clearly showed why Pamela eats so many pretzels.

Eagle Eye
acuity, astute, discern, incisive, keen, perspicacity

BENIGN

adj. <buh-NINE>

_____

_____

_____

_____

BENIGN

kind; beneficial

Mystic Dan reassured Pamela that he is **benign** and only uses remarkable powers for good.

VACILLATE

v. <VAS-uh-layt>

_____

_____

_____

_____

VACILLATE

to be undecided, to hesitate

Pamela **vacillated** and went back and forth about whether to use Mystic Dan's services.

Synonyms: waver

OBSTREPEROUS
adj. <uhb-STREP-er-uhs>

_____

_____

_____

_____

OBSTREPEROUS

noisily and stubbornly defiant

Pamela was **obstreperous**, noisily defiant like a child, when Mystic Dan asked for details about Laura.

Noise Pollution
boisterous, cacophony, obstreperous, tumultuous

BELITTLE
v. <bi-LIT-il>

_____

_____

_____

_____

BELITTLE

to speak of in an insulting way

Pamela and Laura **belittle** people as they walk by, speaking insultingly about their appearance.

Trash Talk
belittle, decry, denigrate, denounce, deprecate, deride, disparage, vilify

---

VOLUMINOUS
adj. <vuh-LOO-muh-nuhs>

_____

_____

_____

_____

VOLUMINOUS

big; having large volume

Pamela's **voluminous** diary is very, very large.

Synonyms: copious, prodigious

ARCHAIC
adj. <ar-KAY-ik>

_____

_____

_____

_____

ARCHAIC

outdated; really old

Laura's **ancient** Roman spear was an old, archaic eating utensil.

Old School
archaic, obsolete

Word Alert: If *-ology* means *study of* then what would *archeology* mean?

PATRONIZE
v. <PAY-truh-nize>

_____

_____

_____

_____

PATRONIZE

to treat condescendingly

Mystic Dan was **patronizing** to Pamela, treating her condescendingly when he heard she had a blog.

Cocky
bombastic, condescend, grandiose, haughty, patronize, pompous, pretentious

INCONTROVERTIBLE
adj. <in-kon-truh-VUR-tuh-buhl>

_____

_____

_____

_____

INCONTROVERTIBLE

impossible to dispute

Pamela's book deal was **incontrovertible**; her document signed in blood made it impossible to dispute.

PRECARIOUS
adj. <pri-KAIR-ee-uhs>

_____

_____

_____

_____

PRECARIOUS

dangerously unstable or insecure

Pamela's life without a best friend, like the dangerously unstable egg on the edge of the table, was **precarious**.

DISMISS
v. <dis-MIS>

_____

_____

_____

_____

DISMISS

to reject

Pamela **dismissed** Mystic Dan's advice; she rejected his wisdom and tore up the paper.

Word Alert: Someone *dismissive* tends to dismiss everything.

OBSTINATE
adj. <OB-stuh-nit>

_____

_____

_____

_____

OBSTINATE

stubborn

Pamela is **obstinate** and stubbornly refuses to apologize to Laura.

Pig-Headed
dogged, dogmatic, intransigent, obdurate, obstinate, tenacity

DISSIPATE
v. <DIS-uh-payt>

_____

_____

_____

_____

_____

DISSIPATE

to disappear

Mystic Dan **dissipated** before Pamela's eyes, disappearing into thin air.

CIRCUMVENT
v. <sur-kuhm-VENT>

_____

_____

_____

_____

INDIGNATION
n. <in-dig-NAY-shun>

_____

_____

_____

_____

PENITENT
adj. <PEN-i-tuhnt>

_____

_____

_____

_____

GENIAL
adj. <JEEN-ee-uhl>

_____

_____

_____

_____

INCORRIGIBLE
adj. <in-KOR-i-juh-buhl>

_____

_____

_____

_____

CIRCUMVENT

to avoid or get around

Pamela **circumvented** Laura by taking a roundabout path and managed to avoid her.

Synonyms: elude [see elusive], evade [see evasive]

INDIGNATION

anger (over something unjust)

Laura became **indignant** when Pamela tried to apologize, expressing her anger over Pamela's unjust behavior.

Word Alert: To be *indignant* is to feel indignation.

PENITENT

feeling or expressing remorse

Pamela was **penitent** and apologized for all the bad things she's done to Laura.

Synonyms: contrite

Word Alert: *Penitence* is the state of being penitent. A *penance* is an act of penitence.

GENIAL

friendly, cheerful

After Pamela apologizes, she and Laura become **genial** again and go back to being best friends.

BFF
amiable, affable, amicable, camaraderie, cordial, genial

Word Alert: *Congenial* also means friendly or sociable.

INCORRIGIBLE

incapable of being corrected or reformed

Pamela is **incorrigible** about insulting people and can never change her ways.

Rumor Chick: The New Guy

Pamela and Kristin are jealous of Laura's new study partner and will stop at nothing to steal him away.

ASSIDUOUS	hard working
OMINOUS	menacing; threatening
QUELL	to put down forcibly
MANIFEST	to make evident or certain by displaying or demonstrating
BEMUSE	to confuse, stun, or stump
ESTRANGE	to cause to become unfriendly or hostile
SUPPLANT	to take the place of
NOTORIOUS	known widely and unfavorably; famous for something bad
ADULATION	excessive flattery
ADMONISH	to gently criticize or warn
CONCUR	to agree
COMPLICITY	participation in a bad act or a crime
POIGNANT	touching
CUNNING	clever, sneaky
ASCERTAIN	to discover
MOROSE	gloomy
REBUKE	to criticize or find fault with
RECIPROCATE	to show or give in return
RENOUNCE	to reject, disown, or formally give up
CONCEDE	to acknowledge, often reluctantly, as being true

ASSIDUOUS
adj. <uh-SIJ-oo-uhs>

_____

_____

_____

_____

ASSIDUOUS

hard working

Laura **assiduously** studied her flashcards, working hard late into the night.

Synonyms: diligent

OMINOUS
adj. <OM-uh-nuhs>

_____

_____

_____

_____

OMINOUS

menacing; threatening

The caller's voice was **ominous** and Laura sensed she might be in danger.

QUELL
v. <KWEL>

_____

_____

_____

_____

QUELL

to put down forcibly

Laura **quelled** the intruder's attack, stopping his advances by knocking him down with the bedroom door.

Synonyms: subdue, suppress

MANIFEST
v. <MAN-uh-fest>

_____

_____

_____

_____

MANIFEST

to make evident or certain by displaying or demonstrating

The intruder **manifests** his identity to Laura by showing her his driver's license.

Word Alert: Manifest can also be an adjective meaning *clearly apparent to the mind or senses.*
Word Alert: A *manifesto* is a written document in which you reveal your beliefs.

BEMUSE
v. <bih-MYOOZ>

_____

_____

_____

_____

_____

BEMUSE

to confuse, stun, or stump

Pamela and Kirsten were **bemused** by the new guy's decision to date Laura - they just couldn't understand it.

Synonyms: confound

ESTRANGE
v. <ih-STRANGE>

_____

_____

_____

_____

ESTRANGE

to cause to become unfriendly or hostile

Pamela and Laura are **estranged**, they used to be friends but now they are hostile towards each other.

Synonyms: alienate

SUPPLANT
v. <suh-PLANT>

_____

_____

_____

_____

SUPPLANT

to take the place of

Pamela plans to **supplant** Laura by taking her place as the Study Partner's girlfriend.

NOTORIOUS
adj. <no-TAWR-ee-uhs>

_____

_____

_____

_____

NOTORIOUS

known widely and unfavorably; famous for something bad

Pamela and Kirsten are **notorious** at school; everyone knows that they like to ruin people's lives.

Word Alert: Notoriety is the state of being notorious.

ADULATION
n. <AJ-uh-lay-tion>

_____

_____

_____

_____

ADULATION

excessive flattery

The first step in Pamela's master plan was **adulation**: excessively flattering the Study Partner for his vocabulary skills.

Hip Hip Hooray!
acclaim, adulation, commend, exalt, extol, laud

ADMONISH
v. <ad-MON-ish>

_____

_____

_____

_____

ADMONISH

to gently criticize or warn

Laura **admonished** the Study Partner, gently warning him not to study with Pamela and Kirsten.

Thumbs Down
admonish, berate, censure, rebuke, reproach, scathing

CONCUR

v. <kuhn-KUR>

_____

_____

_____

_____

CONCUR

to agree

Pamela and Kirsten **concur** that they should set Laura up, and agree to set a trap for her.

Like-Minded
accord, concord, concur, conform, consensus, uniform

COMPLICITY

n. <kuhm-PLIS-i-tee>

_____

_____

_____

_____

COMPLICITY

participation in a bad act or a crime

Doug is **complicit** in Pamela and Kirstin's scheme, he willingly participates in their evil plan.

POIGNANT

adj. <POIN-yuhnt>

_____

_____

_____

_____

POIGNANT

touching

Doug's **poignant** plea to Laura was so touching that he convinced her to help him study.

CUNNING

adj. <KUHN-ing>

_____

_____

_____

_____

CUNNING

clever, sneaky

The girls were **cunning**, sneakily taking pictures of Laura to set her up.

Shady
cunning, duplicity, guile, treachery

Word Alert: Cunning can also be a noun meaning *skillful deception.*

ASCERTAIN

v. <ASS-er-tain>

_____

_____

_____

_____

ASCERTAIN

to discover

The Study Partner **ascertains** that Laura has been unfaithful, he sees the photos and discovers she's been studying with another guy.

MOROSE
adj. <muh-ROHS>

_____

_____

_____

_____

MOROSE

gloomy

The Study Partner became **morose** and gloomy after he discovered that Laura had been studying with someone else.

Cry Baby
despair, despondent, dour, lament, melancholy, morose

REBUKE
v. <ri-BYOOK>

_____

_____

_____

_____

REBUKE

to criticize or find fault with

The Study Partner **rebuked** Laura, criticizing her for studying vocab with someone else.

Thumbs Down
admonish, berate, censure, rebuke, reproach, scathing

Word Alert: Rebuke can also be a noun meaning *an act or expression of criticism.*

RECIPROCATE
v. <ri-SIP-ruh-kayt>

_____

_____

_____

_____

RECIPROCATE

to show or give in return

The Study Partner **reciprocates** Laura's infidelity, in return he betrays her and studies with Pamela.

RENOUNCE
v. <ri-NOUNCE>

_____

_____

_____

_____

RENOUNCE

to reject, disown, or formally give up

Laura **renounced** her friendship with Pamela, formally declaring that they are no longer friends.

Synonyms: relinquish

Word Alert: A *renunciation* is an act of renouncing.

CONCEDE
v. <kuhn-SEED>

_____

_____

_____

_____

CONCEDE

to acknowledge, often reluctantly, as being true

Doug **concedes** the argument to the Study Partner, acknowledging that girls are great after all.

Word Alert: A *concession* is the act of conceding.

SHALL WE DANCE? PART 1

Hoping to spice up his life Dudley enrolls in dance classes while Hank volunteers to make a documentary.

BANAL	ordinary and commonplace
DISPOSITION	one's usual mood
IMPASSIONED	filled with passion
ENTICE	to lure
CONTRIVED	obviously planned or made up
EMBELLISH	to add fictitious details to
DEPRECATE	to mildly insult or belittle
OBTUSE	lacking intellect
TUMULTUOUS	disorderly or noisy
INDIFFERENT	having no preference
CONVIVIAL	sociable
RETICENT	restrained or reserved
VIVACIOUS	lively
ESOTERIC	understood by only a few
FACILITATE	to make easier
AFFABLE	friendly
STAGNANT	not moving, flowing, or developing
TRIVIAL	insignificant, unimportant
PARTISAN	devoted to or biased in support of a group
COMPETENT	having adequate ability

BANAL
adj. <buh-NAL or BAY-nul>

_____

_____

_____

_____

BANAL

ordinary and commonplace

Because he had the same routine everyday, the office had become **banal** for Dudley.

Played Out
banal, hackneyed, insipid, mundane, prosaic, trite

DISPOSITION
n. <dis-puh-ZIH-shuhn>

_____

_____

_____

_____

DISPOSITION

one's usual mood

Hank noticed that Dudley's **disposition** had changed; he was not being his normal self.

IMPASSIONED
adj. <im-PASH-uhnd>

_____

_____

_____

_____

IMPASSIONED

filled with passion

Displaying intense emotion, Hank gave Dudley an **impassioned** speech about his love for money.

X-treme Intensity!
ardor, fervent, galvanize, impassioned, zealous

ENTICE
v. <en-TICE>

_____

_____

_____

_____

ENTICE

to lure

Dudley imagined that the dance instructor was **enticing** him into the studio, luring him to follow her.

CONTRIVED
adj. <kuhn-TRAHYVD>

_____

_____

_____

_____

CONTRIVED

obviously planned or made up

Dudley's explanation was clearly **contrived**, an obvious and artificial story.

EMBELLISH

v. <em-BEL-ish>

_____

_____

_____

_____

EMBELLISH

to add fictitious details to

Hank **embellished** his film-making skills, exaggerating his experience so that his boss would ask him to make the video.

Synonyms: adorn

DEPRECATE

v. <DEP-ruh-kate>

_____

_____

_____

_____

DEPRECATE

to mildly insult or belittle

Hank **deprecated** Dudley for sleeping on the job, criticizing him for his lack of effort.

Trash Talk
belittle, decry, denigrate, denounce, deprecate, deride, disparage, vilify

---

OBTUSE

adj. <uhb-TOOS>

_____

_____

_____

_____

OBTUSE

lacking intellect

Dudley was truly **obtuse** while operating the video camera; he could not find the record button and forgot to take the lens cover off.

Synonyms: fatuous

TUMULTUOUS

adj. <too-MUHL-choo-uhs>

_____

_____

_____

_____

TUMULTUOUS

disorderly or noisy

The scene in the dance studio was **tumultuous**: disorderly, noisy and full of loud music and relentless phone calls.

Noise Pollution
boisterous, cacophony, obstreperous, tumultuous

Word Alert: A *tumult* is a tumultuous occurrence.

INDIFFERENT

adj. <in-DIF-er-ent>

_____

_____

_____

_____

INDIFFERENT

having no preference

Dudley was **indifferent** about which dance to choose; he had no preference as long as Miss Linda was teaching it.

Synonyms: apathetic, nonchalant

Word Alert: This word does NOT mean *not different.*

CONVIVIAL
adj. <kuhn-VIV-ee-uhl>

_____

_____

_____

_____

CONVIVIAL

sociable

Gary's **convivial** and sociable nature was immediately evident as he enthusiastically introduced himself to Dudley and Miss Linda.

Synonyms: gregarious

RETICENT
adj. <RET-uh-suhn>t

_____

_____

_____

_____

RETICENT

restrained or reserved

Dudley was **reticent** when Miss Linda asked him to dance, so reserved that he barely appeared to be dancing at all.

Tight-Lipped
concise, laconic, reticent, succinct, terse

VIVACIOUS
adj. <vi-VAY-shuhs>

_____

_____

_____

_____

VIVACIOUS

lively

Miss Linda explained to Dudley and Gary that they must be **vivacious** when they dance, full of energy and life.

Party Hearty!
ebullient, exuberant, vivacious

ESOTERIC
adj. <es-uh-TER-ik>

_____

_____

_____

_____

ESOTERIC

understood by only a few

Miss Linda's explanation of an **esoteric** style of dance left Dudley and Gary confused; it could only be understood by the few who have studied it.

What the—?
abstruse, ambiguous, amorphous, enigmatic, equivocal, esoteric, nebulous

---

FACILITATE
v. <fuh-SIL-i-tayt>

_____

_____

_____

_____

FACILITATE

to make easier

Miss Linda's use of bubble wrap **facilitated** the lesson, making it easier for the class to learn.

Word Alert: Something *facile* is easy or done with little difficulty.

AFFABLE
adj. <AF-uh-buhl>

_____

_____

_____

_____

AFFABLE

friendly

Dudley went to the office after dance class with a new, **affable** attitude; he was exceptionally friendly to all of his co-workers.

BFF
amiable, affable, amicable, camaraderie, cordial, genial

STAGNANT
adj. <STAG-nuhnt>

_____

_____

_____

_____

STAGNANT

not moving, flowing, or developing

Hank used the graph to illustrate how many careers become **stagnant** after five years at a company, with no possibility of promotion or development.

Word Alert: To *stagnate* is to become stagnant.

TRIVIAL
adj. <TRIV-ee-uhl>

_____

_____

_____

_____

TRIVIAL

insignificant, unimportant

Hank's tour of the lesser-known wing of the office only uncovers **trivial** and unimportant rooms like the paper storage room.

Synonyms: frivolous, inconsequential, negligible

Word Alert: To *trivialize* is to make something seem trivial.

PARTISAN
adj. <PAHR-tuh-zuhn>

_____

_____

_____

_____

PARTISAN

devoted to or biased in support of a group

Hank's co-workers were **partisan** in their answers, clearly biased in their support of the company.

Word Alert: If the prefix *non-* means *not*, what would *nonpartisan* mean?

COMPETENT
adj. <KOM-pi-tuhnt>

_____

_____

_____

_____

COMPETENT

having adequate ability

Despite his exaggerated claims, Hank turned out to be a **competent** filmmaker, proving he had the ability to make a good documentary.

Word Alert: If the prefix *in-* means *not*, what would *incompetent* mean?

SHALL WE DANCE? PART 2

Dudley and his new friend Gary try to convince their instructor, Miss Linda, to dance competitively.

CONFORM	to be similar; to adapt
PROPRIETY	the quality of being proper
CONSTRAIN	to hold back; to restrict
INNATE	inborn
WAVER	to be unsure or weak
UNIFORM	always the same
INSINUATE	to suggest subtly; to hint
PERPETUAL	continuing forever or indefinitely
CEREBRAL	intellectual
WHIMSICAL	impulsive, fanciful
SQUANDER	to waste
ADVERSITY	great hardship
PERTINENT	exactly relevant
AUSTERE	strict or severe in discipline
ABSTRUSE	difficult to understand
CLANDESTINE	kept or done in secret
CONDONE	to excuse or overlook
OFFICIOUS	overly eager in offering unwanted help
DISCREPANCY	an unexpected difference
EMINENT	outstanding; distinguished

CONFORM

v. <kuhn-FORM>

_____

_____

_____

_____

CONFORM

to be similar; to adapt

Gary must **conform** to the cruise line's rules; he has to adapt to their requirements and rehearse a line each time he asks a guest to dance.

Like-Minded
accord, concord, concur, conform, consensus, uniform

Word Alert: When you conform, you put yourself in a state of *conformity*.

PROPRIETY

n. <pruh-PRY-i-tee>

_____

_____

_____

_____

PROPRIETY

the quality of being proper

Unlike Gary, Dudley acts with **propriety** when he dances with Miss Linda; his conduct is proper and correct.

Word Alert: If *im-* means *not*, what would *impropriety* mean?

CONSTRAIN

v. <kuhn-STRAYN>

_____

_____

_____

_____

CONSTRAIN

to hold back; to restrict

Miss Linda instructs Dudley to **constrain** Gary's arms, restricting them so that Gary can focus on his dance steps.

Word Alert: A *constraint* is something that constrains.

INNATE

adj. <ih-NAYT>

_____

_____

_____

_____

INNATE

inborn

Miss Linda has an **innate** talent for dance; since many of her family members were dancers, she was born with her exceptional ability.

Synonyms: inherent

WAVER

v. <WAY-ver>

_____

_____

_____

_____

WAVER

to be unsure or weak

Unsure of himself, Dudley **wavered** when Miss Linda asked him to dance.

Synonyms: vacillate

UNIFORM
adj. <YOO-nuh-form>

_____

_____

_____

_____

UNIFORM

always the same

When Dudley and Gary practice the waltz, their steps must be **uniform**: exactly the same every time.

Like-Minded
accord, concord, concur, conform, consensus, uniform

INSINUATE
v. <in-SIN-yoo-ate>

_____

_____

_____

_____

INSINUATE

to suggest subtly; to hint

Hinting that he knows why Dudley is unusually happy, Hank **insinuated** that he is involved in some kind of profitable project outside the office.

PERPETUAL
adj. <per-PEH-choo-uhl>

_____

_____

_____

_____

PERPETUAL

continuing forever or indefinitely

Hank warns Dudley about the **perpetual** struggle of dealing with women and rejection, describing it as a never-ending cycle.

Word Alert: To *perpetuate* is to make something perpetual.

CEREBRAL
adj. <suh-REE-brul>

_____

_____

_____

_____

CEREBRAL

intellectual

Miss Linda tells Dudley that his approach to learning dance is too **cerebral**; his intellectual method of memorizing the footwork and studying dance books is not effective.

WHIMSICAL
adj. <WIM-zi-kuhl>

_____

_____

_____

_____

WHIMSICAL

impulsive, fanciful

Miss Linda instructs Dudley to copy Gary's **whimsical**, impulsive dance style as he moves without thinking on the dance floor.

Unpredictable
arbitrary, capricious, erratic, impetuous, mercurial, mutable, volatile, whimsical

Word Alert: A *whim* is a whimsical thought or feeling.

SQUANDER
v. <SKWON-der>

_____

_____

_____

_____

SQUANDER

to waste

Dudley and Gary think that Miss Linda is **squandering** her talent; she is wasting it teaching them when she has the ability to dance professionally.

ADVERSITY
n. <ad-VUR-si-tee>

_____

_____

_____

_____

ADVERSITY

great hardship

Miss Linda tells Dudley and Gary about the **adversity** and hardship that dancers can face; she even has so little money that she has to eat cat food.

Word Alert: Adverse means harmful or contrary.

PERTINENT
adj. <PUR-ti-nuhnt>

_____

_____

_____

_____

PERTINENT

exactly relevant

The "America's Next Best Dancer" flyer was **pertinent** to Miss Linda's life; it was as though it was written specifically for her because it was exactly relevant to her life story.

AUSTERE
adj. <aw-STEER>

_____

_____

_____

_____

AUSTERE

strict or severe in discipline

Angered by Dudley and Gary's proposal, Miss Linda was **austere** for the remainder of the class; she was severe and strict, and ordered her students to face the wall when they didn't get the dance right.

ABSTRUSE
adj. <ab-STROOS>

_____

_____

_____

_____

ABSTRUSE

difficult to understand

The specifications Gary gave Dudley about the camera were **abstruse**, very difficult for anyone unfamiliar with cameras to really understand.

What the—?
abstruse, ambiguous, amorphous, enigmatic, equivocal, esoteric, nebulous

CLANDESTINE
adj. <clan-DEHS-tin>

_____

_____

_____

_____

CLANDESTINE

kept or done in secret

Dudley takes Hank's camera in a **clandestine** fashion; he does it in secret so Hank won't find out.

Synonyms: surreptitious

CONDONE
v. <kuhn-DOHN>

_____

_____

_____

_____

CONDONE

to excuse or overlook

Hank **condones** Dudley's sneaky behavior, overlooking his theft once he sees the beautiful Miss Linda dancing.

OFFICIOUS
adj. <uh-FISH-uhs>

_____

_____

_____

_____

OFFICIOUS

overly eager in offering unwanted help

Overly eager to help in any way, Hank was proving to be **officious**.

Synonyms: obtrusive

DISCREPANCY
n. <di-SKREP-uhn-see>

_____

_____

_____

_____

DISCREPANCY

an unexpected difference

There is a **discrepancy** between what Hank initially said about his "date" and what he says when Dudley questions him, as he offers different answers each time.

Synonyms: disparity

EMINENT
adj. <EM-uh-nuhnt>

_____

_____

_____

_____

EMINENT

outstanding; distinguished

Dudley, Gary, and Hank agree that Miss Linda is an **eminent** dancer, outstanding in her ability and true "ballroom dancing royalty."

SHALL WE DANCE? PART 3

After Hank joins the class, the dancers prepare tirelessly for a big performance.

DISSEMBLE	to conceal behind a false appearance
CYNICAL	believing that people are motivated by selfishness; pessimistic
TORPOR	inactivity
EPHEMERAL	lasting for a brief time
DISCREDIT	to bring shame or dishonor on
TACT	sensitivity in dealing with others
PREDILECTION	a preference; a tendency toward favoring
MIRTH	gladness, amusement, laughter
INHIBIT	to hold back; to restrain
DISPASSIONATE	not influenced by emotion or bias
CORROBORATE	to strengthen or support with evidence
INCONSEQUENTIAL	lacking importance
ARTICULATE	characterized by clear and expressive language
POLARIZE	to set at opposite ends or extremes
TENACITY	persistence, determination
CAUSTIC	harsh, stinging; sarcastic
BOISTEROUS	noisy; disorderly
COGENT	forcefully convincing
LATENT	existing in hidden or dormant form
ADEPT	very skilled

DISSEMBLE
v. <di-SEM-buhl>

_____

_____

_____

_____

DISSEMBLE

to conceal behind a false appearance

Hank **dissembled** his real identity, concealing it behind a false name and a fake moustache.

don't confuse this word with disassemble

CYNICAL
adj. <SIN-ih-cul>

_____

_____

_____

_____

CYNICAL

believing that people are motivated by selfishness; pessimistic

Hank's attitude was pessimistic and **cynical**: he believed that his co-workers would tell his boss about the dance classes costing him a promotion.

Word Alert: A *cynic* is a cynical person who is full of *cynicism*

TORPOR
n. <TOR-per>

_____

_____

_____

_____

TORPOR

inactivity

Miss Linda tries to rouse Hank from the **torpor** of his lazy life, encouraging him to be active and show off his dance skills.

Word Alert: To be *torpid* is to possess torpor.

EPHEMERAL
adj. <eh-FEE-muh-ral>

_____

_____

_____

_____

EPHEMERAL

lasting for a brief time

Dudley's perfect waltz with Miss Linda is **ephemeral**, as Hank interrupts causing Dudley to injure her.

Gone with the Wind
elusive, ephemeral, evanescent, evasive, transient, transitory

---

DISCREDIT
v. <dis-KRED-it>

_____

_____

_____

_____

DISCREDIT

to bring shame or dishonor on

Dudley **discredited** Hank by revealing in front of Miss Linda that his claim to be a Broadway dancer was false.

TACT
n. <rhymes with *fact*>

_____

_____

_____

_____

TACT

sensitivity in dealing with others

Miss Linda showed great **tact** and sensitivity when dealing with a very upset Hank and his feelings.

PREDILECTION
n. <pred-ih-LEK-shuhn>

_____

_____

_____

_____

PREDILECTION

a preference; a tendency toward favoring

Hank has a **predilection** for rap music, preferring hip-hop to the classical tune.

Synonyms: propensity

MIRTH
n. <rhymes with *birth*>

_____

_____

_____

_____

MIRTH

gladness, amusement, laughter

Hank's amusing dance moves brought **mirth** and laughter to everyone in the studio.

Happy Camper
buoyant, ecstasy, elated, euphoria, felicity, mirth, sanguine

---

INHIBIT
v. <in-HIB-it>

_____

_____

_____

_____

INHIBIT

to hold back; to restrain

Miss Linda instructs Dudley and Gary to **inhibit** the movement of Hank's hips using rope, restraining his movements so that can learn to waltz.

Road Block
hamper, hinder, impede, inhibit, thwart

DISPASSIONATE
adj. <dis-PASH-uh-nit>

_____

_____

_____

_____

DISPASSIONATE

not influenced by emotion or bias

Dudley gave a **dispassionate** assessment of Miss Linda's dancing; unlike Hank and Gary, he didn't let his emotions influence his judgment.

Synonyms: impartial

CORROBORATE

v. <kuh-ROB-uh-rayt>

_____

_____

_____

_____

CORROBORATE

to strengthen or support with evidence

Hank **corroborates** Scott's claim that Dudley was dancing in the kitchen, supporting it by showing him Dudley's book, "The Magic of Dance."

INCONSEQUENTIAL

adj. <in-kon-si-KWEN-shuhl>

_____

_____

_____

_____

INCONSEQUENTIAL

lacking importance

Scott's opinion of him was **inconsequential** to Dudley, who was much more concerned with preparing for dance class.

Synonyms: frivolous, negligible, trivial

Word Alert: Consequential means important, or having a consequence.

ARTICULATE

adj. <ahr-TIK-yuh-lit>

_____

_____

_____

_____

ARTICULATE

characterized by clear and expressive language

Dudley and Gary could not find the words to explain it clearly, but Miss Linda was **articulate** describing exactly what Hank was doing wrong on the dance floor.

Synonyms: eloquent

Word Alert: Articulate can also be a verb meaning to speak or pronounce distinctly.

POLARIZE

v. <POH-luh-rize>

_____

_____

_____

_____

POLARIZE

to set at opposite ends or extremes

The debate over whether to go to in the fireman's ball **polarized** the dancers; Miss Linda and Gary wanted to perform, but Dudley and Hank felt the opposite.

Word Alert: To be polar is to be at opposite ends.

TENACITY

n. <tuh-NAS-ih-tee>

_____

_____

_____

_____

TENACITY

persistence, determination

Rather than give up when confronted by difficulty, Dudley, Gary, and Hank displayed tremendous **tenacity** preparing for the performance.

Pig-Headed
dogged, dogmatic, intransigent, obdurate, obstinate, tenacity

Word Alert: To be tenacious is to have tenacity.

CAUSTIC
adj. <KAW-stik>

_____

_____

_____

_____

CAUSTIC

harsh, stinging; sarcastic

Hank directed **caustic** insults at Scott; indeed, the stinging and sarcastic words quickly made him leave.

BOISTEROUS
adj. <BOY-ster-uhs>

_____

_____

_____

_____

BOISTEROUS

noisy; disorderly

The dancers were **boisterous** backstage when they heard Miss Linda had been accepted to compete in "America's Next Best Dancer," becoming even louder when they found out that she was not going to participate.

Noise Pollution
boisterous, cacophony, obstreperous, tumultuous

COGENT
adj. <KOH-juhnt>

_____

_____

_____

_____

COGENT

forcefully convincing

Although Miss Linda did not want to compete, the students provided a **cogent** and forcefully convincing argument to change her mind.

LATENT
adj. <LAY-tunt>

_____

_____

_____

_____

LATENT

existing in hidden or dormant form

Miss Linda reminded Dudley, Hank, and Gary of their **latent** talent for dance; it had been hidden within them and now they have let it free.

ADEPT
adj. <uh-DEPT>

_____

_____

_____

_____

ADEPT

very skilled

Under Miss Linda's instruction, Dudley, Gary, and Hank have become **adept** dancers, and their performance at the fireman's ball proved just how skillful they now are.

Synonyms: adroit

THE ARTISTS PART 1

Determined to become a great painter, George visits the studio of Rene the master artist.

ECCENTRIC	strange; unconventional
VENERATE	to respect
OPAQUE	not clearly understood; dense
EMULATE	to equal through imitation
ABSTINENCE	deliberate self-restraint
TRANQUIL	calm
AESTHETIC	concerning beauty
AMALGAM	a combination of diverse elements
MUTABLE	subject to change
CANDID	honest and straightforward
ACERBIC	bitter
AUTONOMY	independence
BELIE	to represent falsely
RECLUSIVE	seeking or preferring isolation
NOSTALGIA	a bittersweet longing for the past
ENTHRALL	to hold spellbound, captivate
COLLABORATE	to work together
GALVANIZE	to stimulate
ABHOR	to hate
INNOVATIVE	new and creative

ECCENTRIC
adj. <ek-SEN-trik>

_____

_____

_____

_____

ECCENTRIC

strange; unconventional

René's odd behavior and appearance show how **eccentric** he is.

Word Alert: An *eccentricity* is an eccentric characteristic.

VENERATE
v. <VEN-uh-rayt>

_____

_____

_____

_____

VENERATE

to respect

George the apprentice **venerates** his master René and showed him great respect.

Word Alert: Something *venerable* is worthy of veneration.

OPAQUE
adj. <oh-PAKE>

_____

_____

_____

_____

OPAQUE

not clearly understood; dense

The intended meaning of René's painting is **opaque**, George cannot figure it out.

Word Alert: Opacity is the state of being opaque.

EMULATE
v. <EM-yuh-layt>

_____

_____

_____

_____

EMULATE

to equal through imitation

Rather than develop his own style, George chooses to **emulate** René.

ABSTINENCE
n. <AB-stuh-nuhns>

_____

_____

_____

_____

ABSTINENCE

deliberate self-restraint

George has exercised **abstinence** by not eating.

TRANQUIL
adj. <TRAN-kwil>

_____

_____

_____

_____

TRANQUIL

calm

René is **tranquil**; he is a calm, peaceful state.

Chill
composed, equanimity, placid, serene, tranquil

Word Alert: *Tranquility* is the state of being tranquil. A *tranquilizer* is a drug that makes you tranquil.

AESTHETIC
adj. <ess-THEH-tik>

_____

_____

_____

_____

AESTHETIC

concerning beauty

René emphasizes **aesthetic** matters and urges George to appreciate the beauty of everyday things.

Word Alert: An *aesthete* is a person who is very concerned with aesthetic things.

AMALGAM
n. <uh-MAL-gum>

_____

_____

_____

_____

AMALGAM

a combination of diverse elements

George's painting is an **amalgam** of many different colors.

Word Alert: To *amalgamate* is to make an amalgam.

MUTABLE
adj. <MYOO-tuh-buhl>

_____

_____

_____

_____

MUTABLE

subject to change

George's interpretations are **mutable**; his description of the painting is always changing.

Unpredictable
arbitrary, capricious, erratic, impetuous, mercurial, mutable, volatile, whimsical

Word Alert: If the prefix *im-* means *not*, what would *immutable* mean?

CANDID
adj. <KAN-did>

_____

_____

_____

_____

CANDID

honest and straightforward

René is **candid** in his open and honest criticism of George's paintings.

Synonyms: ingenuous, forthright

Word Alert: *Candor* is the quality of being candid.

ACERBIC
adj. <uh-SER-bik>

_____

_____

_____

_____

ACERBIC

bitter

George becomes **acerbic** and bitterly lashes out when he realizes he is not a good painter.

AUTONOMY
n. <aw-TAWN-uh-mee>

_____

_____

_____

_____

AUTONOMY

independence

George establishes his **autonomy** by going out on his own and leaving René behind.

Word Alert: Someone *autonomous* possesses autonomy.

BELIE
v. <beh-LYE>

_____

_____

_____

_____

BELIE

to represent falsely

René's words **belie** the truth: despite what he says, he really misses George.

RECLUSIVE
adj. <ri-KLOOS-iv>

_____

_____

_____

_____

RECLUSIVE

seeking or preferring isolation

After George left, René became **reclusive** and refused to speak to anyone.

Word Alert: A *recluse* is someone who is reclusive.

NOSTALGIA
n. <no-STAL-juh>

_____

_____

_____

_____

NOSTALGIA

a bittersweet longing for the past

René feels **nostalgic** and dreams about his time with George.

Synonyms:

Word Alert: If you are *nostalgic*, you are experiencing nostalgia.

ENTHRALL
v. <en-THRAWL>

_____

_____

_____

_____

ENTHRALL

to hold spellbound, captivate

René is **enthralled** by George's captivating appearance.

COLLABORATE
v. <kuh-LAB-uh-rayt>

_____

_____

_____

_____

COLLABORATE

to work together

George wants to **collaborate** with René to make a lot of money together.

GALVANIZE
v. <GAL-vuh-nize>

_____

_____

_____

_____

GALVANIZE

to stimulate

George **galvanizes** René to get excited about painting again.

X-treme Intensity!
ardor, fervent, galvanize, impassioned, zealous

ABHOR
v. <ab-HOR>

_____

_____

_____

_____

ABHOR

to hate

George **abhors** René's work and thinks it's all terrible.

Bad Blood
abhor, acrimony, animosity, antagonistic, contempt, disdain, enmity, rancor, scorn

Word Alert: *Abhorrence* is the feeling of abhorring.

INNOVATIVE
adj. <IN-uh-vay-tiv>

_____

_____

_____

_____

INNOVATIVE

new and creative

René's **innovative** painting is totally different from any other artwork.

Synonyms: novel

Word Alert: To *innovate* is to be innovative. An *innovation* is an innovative creation.

THE ARTISTS PART 2

René and George resort to desperate measures to sell paintings and are saved by a passerby.

MEAGER	small, inadequate, or insufficient
DELINEATE	to depict or describe
CONCISE	expressing much in few words
EFFICACIOUS	effective
ACCORD	agreement
DUBIOUS	doubtful, questionable
LAUD	to praise
ANTAGONISTIC	hostile
BERATE	to criticize severely or angrily
AWE	a mixed emotion of wonder, respect, and dread

MEAGER
adj. <MEEG-er>

_____

_____

_____

_____

MEAGER

small, inadequate, or insufficient

The **meager** dinner of the remains of a deli sandwich René offered is much too small to satisfy George.

DELINEATE
v. <de-LIN-ee-ate>

_____

_____

_____

_____

DELINEATE

to depict or describe

René **delineated** a plan for how to make money, mapping out the strategy step by step.

CONCISE
adj. <kuhn-SICE>

_____

_____

_____

_____

CONCISE

expressing much in few words

George's sign was **concise**: it got exactly to the point without wasting words.

Tight-Lipped
concise, laconic, reticent, succinct, terse

EFFICACIOUS
adj. <ef-i-KAY-shuhs>

_____

_____

_____

_____

EFFICACIOUS

effective

The sign is **efficacious**, working almost immediately to find the rich person they were seeking.

ACCORD
n. <uh-KORD>

_____

_____

_____

_____

ACCORD

agreement

Hank signs an **accord**, agreeing to pay $1,000 for René to paint his portrait.

Like-Minded
accord, concord, concur, conform, consensus, uniform

Word Alert: Accord can also be a verb meaning *to agree.*

DUBIOUS
adj. <DOO-bee-uhs>

_____

_____

_____

_____

DUBIOUS

doubtful, questionable

Hank is **dubious** and doesn't believe that René is actually a famous European painter.

LAUD
v. <LAWD>

_____

_____

_____

_____

LAUD

to praise

René **lauded** Hank's appearance, praising him to win back his trust.

Hip Hip Hooray!
acclaim, adulation, commend, exalt, extol, laud

Word Alert: Laud has the same root as *applaud.*

ANTAGONISTIC
adj. <an-tag-uh-NIS-tik>

_____

_____

_____

_____

ANTAGONISTIC

hostile

René and Hank quickly become **antagonistic** towards one another and start to argue.

Bad Blood
abhor, acrimony, animosity, antagonistic, contempt, disdain, enmity, rancor, scorn

Word Alert: An *antagonist* is a person who is antagonistic.

BERATE
v. <bi-RAYT>

_____

_____

_____

_____

BERATE

to criticize severely or angrily

George angrily **berates** René for almost ruining their plan, criticizing him for his stupidity.

Thumbs Down
admonish, berate, censure, rebuke, reproach, scathing

AWE
n. <rhymes with *saw*>

_____

_____

_____

_____

AWE

a mixed emotion of wonder, respect, and dread

Hank is in **awe** of René's portrait; he is captivated by its incredible beauty.

Word Alert: Something that causes awe is *awesome.*

STRANDED! PART 1

Brett and Katie find themselves stranded on a desert island and their relationship quickly becomes strained.

SERENE	calm
RUDIMENTARY	being or involving basic facts or principles
EMPIRICAL	based on observation or experiment
OBLIVIOUS	forgetful; unaware
RESENT	to feel angry and bitter about
EFFACE	to erase
CONSOLIDATE	to combine
FATUOUS	foolish, ridiculously stupid
OBSOLETE	no longer in use or current
ANIMOSITY	bitter hostility
REVOKE	to void by recalling, reversing, or withdrawing
REFUGE	protection or shelter
SCOFF	to express or treat with disrespectful disregard
USURP	to seize and take control without authority and possibly with force
UNDERMINE	to weaken
EXASPERATE	to anger or irritate
FLOURISH	to grow well
RECONCILE	to reestablish a close relationship between
EXPLOIT	to utilize fully or advantageously (often selfishly or unethically)
VOLATILE	explosive, tending to change

SERENE
adj. <suh-REEN>

_____

_____

_____

_____

SERENE

calm

It was calm and **serene** on the island right before Brett regained his senses.

Chill
composed, equanimity, placid, serene, tranquil

Word Alert: *Serenity* is the state of being serene.

RUDIMENTARY
adj. <roo-duh-MEN-tuh-ree>

_____

_____

_____

_____

RUDIMENTARY

being or involving basic facts or principles

Brett doesn't even know **rudimentary** facts like where he is and how he got there.

EMPIRICAL
adj. <em-PIR-i-kuhl>

_____

_____

_____

_____

EMPIRICAL

based on observation or experiment

Brett used the evidence around him to reach some **empirical** conclusions.

OBLIVIOUS
adj. <uh-BLIV-ee-uhs>

_____

_____

_____

_____

OBLIVIOUS

forgetful; unaware

Brett was **oblivious** to his situation; he was even unaware that Katie was sitting next to him the whole time.

Word Alert: *Oblivion* is the state of being completely forgotten.

RESENT
v. <ri-ZENT>

_____

_____

_____

_____

RESENT

to feel angry and bitter about

Katie **resents** Brett, angry for all of the annoying things he did on the plane.

EFFACE
v. <ih-FACE>

_____

_____

_____

_____

EFFACE

to erase

Brett **effaced** Katie's writing, erasing her message by wiping away the sand.

CONSOLIDATE
v. <kuhn-SOL-i-dayt>

_____

_____

_____

_____

CONSOLIDATE

to combine

Brett and Katie **consolidated** their possessions, combining them into a single pile.

FATUOUS
adj. <FAT-choo-uhs>

_____

_____

_____

_____

FATUOUS

foolish, ridiculously stupid

Throwing the flare into the ocean was a **fatuous** decision, a ridiculously stupid idea.

Synonyms: obtuse

OBSOLETE
adj. <OB-suh-leet>

_____

_____

_____

_____

OBSOLETE

no longer in use or current

Katie's walkman is **obsolete**; music technology has advanced significantly since the 1980's.

Old School
archaic, obsolete

ANIMOSITY
n. <an-uh-MOS-i-tee>

_____

_____

_____

_____

_____

ANIMOSITY

bitter hostility

Katie showed **animosity** towards Bret, yelling at him in anger.

Bad Blood
abhor, acrimony, animosity, antagonistic, contempt, disdain, enmity, rancor, scorn

REVOKE
v. <ri-VOHK>

_____

_____

_____

_____

REFUGE
n. <REF-yooj>

_____

_____

_____

_____

SCOFF
v. <rhymes with *off*>

_____

_____

_____

_____

USURP
v. <yoo-SURP>

_____

_____

_____

_____

UNDERMINE
v. <un-der-MINE>

_____

_____

_____

_____

REVOKE

to void by recalling, reversing, or withdrawing

Katie **revoked** her offer to Brett, withdrawing her agreement to share the crackers.

REFUGE

protection or shelter

To protect themselves from the elements, Brett and Katie built **refuges** on the beach.

SCOFF

to express or treat with disrespectful disregard

Katie **scoffed** at Brett's tent, ridiculing his poor craftsmanship.

USURP

to seize and take control without authority and possibly with force

Brett **usurped** Katie's tent, taking her place by force.

UNDERMINE

to weaken

Katie's digging **undermined** the stability of the tent, causing it to collapse.

EXASPERATE
v. <ig-ZAS-puh-rayt>

_____

_____

_____

_____

EXASPERATE

to anger or irritate

Brett is **exasperated**, overwhelmed with frustration because everything keeps going wrong.

Synonyms: grate

FLOURISH
v. <FLUR-ish>

_____

_____

_____

_____

FLOURISH

to grow well

Brett's beard quickly **flourished**, growing fully in just a few short days.

Synonyms: burgeon

RECONCILE
v. <REH-kuhn-sahyl>

_____

_____

_____

_____

RECONCILE

to reestablish a close relationship between

Katie and Brett **reconciled** after being enemies; once Brett apologized they became friendly again.

Word Alert: Reconciliation is the act of reconciling.
Word Alert: Reconcile has the same root as *conciliate*.

EXPLOIT
v. <ek-SPLOIT>

_____

_____

_____

_____

EXPLOIT

to utilize fully or advantageously (often selfishly or unethically)

Katie **exploited** Bret by first using him for entertainment and then demanding a massage, taking advantage of his desire to be friends again.

VOLATILE
adj. <VOL-uh-tuhl>

_____

_____

_____

_____

VOLATILE

explosive, tending to change

Bret's emotions are highly **volatile**; one moment he is calm and the next he explodes in anger.

Unpredictable
arbitrary, capricious, erratic, impetuous, mercurial, mutable, volatile, whimsical

STRANDED! PART 2

Brett is getting hungry and an unexpected arrival prompts some desert island Olympics.

RAVENOUS	violently hungry or greedy
ILLUSORY	based on or producing illusion
FUTILE	having no useful result
IMPASSIVE	having or showing little emotion
TRITE	uninteresting because of overuse
SUBSTANTIATE	to support with proof
LANGUID	lacking energy or spirit
VERBOSE	using more words than necessary
INCONGRUOUS	inappropriate; inconsistent
ARDOR	energy, intensity, enthusiasm
PRISTINE	unspoiled, completely pure
CAJOLE	to persuade by flattery
COMPEL	to exert a strong, irresistible force on
DUPLICITY	deception, deceit
RESOLVE	to make a firm decision about
ACCLAIM	to praise
ADROIT	very skilled
PERSEVERE	to be persistent, refuse to stop
CONCILIATE	to bring peace, quiet, or calm to
OPPORTUNE	suitable, occurring at an appropriate time

RAVENOUS
adj. <RAV-uh-nuhs>

_____

_____

_____

_____

RAVENOUS

violently hungry or greedy

Brett has become **ravenous** after being on a desert island for a year without food.

ILLUSORY
adj. <ih-LOO-zuh-ree>

_____

_____

_____

_____

ILLUSORY

based on or producing illusion

The sandwich Brett made was **illusory**; it was only in his mind.

FUTILE
adj. <FYOOT-il>

_____

_____

_____

_____

FUTILE

having no useful result

Brett's method of catching fish was **futile**; it couldn't possibly work.

IMPASSIVE
adj. <im-PAS-iv>

_____

_____

_____

_____

IMPASSIVE

having or showing little emotion

Even when Brett screamed in her face, Katie was **impassive** and did not react.

Synonyms: stoic

Word Alert: Don't confuse this word with *impassioned*.

TRITE
adj. <rhymes with *white*>

_____

_____

_____

_____

TRITE

uninteresting because of overuse

Brett's idea had become **trite** after he talked about it every day.

Played Out
banal, hackneyed, insipid, mundane, prosaic, trite

SUBSTANTIATE
v. <suhb-STAN-shee-ate>

_____

_____

_____

_____

SUBSTANTIATE

to support with proof

Brett **substantiated** his bold claim about being happy on the island by giving evidence.

Word Alert: To substantiate is to give *substance* to an argument.

LANGUID
adj. <LANG-gwid>

_____

_____

_____

_____

LANGUID

lacking energy or spirit

Brett has become **languid**, feeling faint and weak from not eating or drinking.

Word Alert: Languor is the state of being languid.

VERBOSE
adj. <ver-BOHS>

_____

_____

_____

_____

VERBOSE

using more words than necessary

Brett was **verbose** and excessively wordy when talking about their situation.

Synonyms: bombastic, garrulous, voluble

INCONGRUOUS
adj. <in-CON-grew-us>

_____

_____ .

_____

_____

INCONGRUOUS

inappropriate; inconsistent

It is **incongruous** that Brett has been on the island for a year and hasn't lost any weight.

ARDOR
n. <AHR-der>

_____

_____

_____

_____

ARDOR

energy, intensity, enthusiasm

Brett showed unrestrained **ardor** in his enthusiastic response to finding the meal.

X-treme Intensity!
ardor, fervent, galvanize, impassioned, zealous

Word Alert: Someone *ardent* is full of ardor.

PRISTINE
adj. <PRIS-teen>

_____
_____
_____
_____

PRISTINE

unspoiled, completely pure

The meal was in **pristine** condition, perfectly clean despite having traveled across the ocean.

CAJOLE
v. <kuh-JOHL>

_____
_____
_____
_____

CAJOLE

to persuade by flattery

Brett and Katie **cajoled** each other, using flattery to try and get the food.

COMPEL
v. <kuhm-PEL>

_____
_____
_____
_____

COMPEL

to exert a strong, irresistible force on

Katie hoped that talking about water would **compel** Brett to leave by forcing him to get up to pee.

DUPLICITY
n. <doo-PLIS-i-tee>

_____
_____
_____
_____

DUPLICITY

deception, deceit

Brett used **duplicity** by tricking Katie into thinking he was sleeping.

Shady
cunning, duplicity, guile, treachery

Word Alert: Someone that has duplicity is *duplicitous.*

RESOLVE
v. <ri-ZOLV>

_____
_____
_____
_____

RESOLVE

to make a firm decision about

In need of a decision about how to split up the food, Katie and Brett **resolved** to hold a desert island Olympics.

Word Alert: Resolve can also be a noun meaning *determination.*

ACCLAIM
v. <uh-KLAYM>

_____

_____

_____

_____

ACCLAIM

to praise

Brett **acclaimed** Katie's idea, praising her for coming up with the desert island Olympics.

Hip Hip Hooray!
acclaim, adulation, commend, exalt, extol, laud

ADROIT
adj. <uh-DROIT>

_____

_____

_____

_____

ADROIT

very skilled

Brett was **adroit** at throwing coconuts; he was much better at it than Katie thought he would be.

Synonyms: adept

Word Alert: If the prefix *mal-* means bad, what would *maladroit* mean?

PERSEVERE
v. <pur-suh-VEER>

_____

_____

_____

_____

PERSEVERE

to be persistent, refuse to stop

Despite Brett's attempt to trip her, Katie **persevered** and won the race.

CONCILIATE
v. <kuhn-SIL-ee-ate>

_____

_____

_____

_____

CONCILIATE

to bring peace, quiet, or calm to

Seeing that he was upset, Katie **conciliated** Brett by agreeing to share the food after all.

Synonyms: appease

Word Alert: Conciliate has the same root as *reconcile*.

OPPORTUNE
adj. <op-er-TOON>

_____

_____

_____

_____

OPPORTUNE

suitable, occurring at an appropriate time

The sound of the plane overhead created an **opportune** moment for Brett to eat the food.

Word Alert: An *opportunity* is an opportune circumstance. An *opportunist* is someone who (selfishly) seizes opportunities.

STRANDED! PART 3

We learn how Brett got stranded, while the island reveals some more of its mysteries.

DESPONDENT	depressed, having no hope
BUOYANT	cheerful
COPIOUS	plentiful, abundant
INCREDULOUS	disbelieving
LAMENT	to regret; to show grief for
ENHANCE	to make greater or better
HOMOGENEOUS	all of the same or similar kind
SUPPRESS	to put down; to hold back
EXPEDITE	to speed the progress of
APPREHENSIVE	fearful
DEBUNK	to disprove or expose the falseness of
LACONIC	using few words (often rudely or mysteriously)
VULNERABLE	not protected against harm
EXTOL	to praise
ELUCIDATE	to make clear
NEBULOUS	hazy, vague, or confused
EULOGY	a written or spoken tribute (usually for someone who has died)
SOLEMN	serious and sober
FEASIBLE	possible, workable, practical
EXUBERANT	lively

DESPONDENT
adj. <di-SPON-duhnt>

_____

_____

_____

_____

DESPONDENT

depressed, having no hope

Brett became **despondent** about being on the island and lost all hope of a normal life.

Cry Baby
despair, despondent, dour, lament, melancholy, morose

BUOYANT
adj. <BOY-ant>

_____

_____

_____

_____

BUOYANT

cheerful

Brett was **buoyant** after getting a promotion, skipping and giggling like a school girl all the way home.

Happy Camper
buoyant, ecstasy, elated, euphoria, felicity, mirth, sanguine

---

COPIOUS
adj. <KOH-pee-uhs>

_____

_____

_____

_____

COPIOUS

plentiful, abundant

Brett drank a **copious** amount of orange juice, spilling it all over his face and drenching his shirt.

Synonyms: prodigious, voluminous

INCREDULOUS
adj. <in-KRE-juh-luhs>

_____

_____

_____

_____

INCREDULOUS

disbelieving

Brett is **incredulous** toward the caller and didn't believe he was really a radio dj.

Synonyms: skeptical

Word Alert: Don't confuse this word with *incredible*.
Word Alert: *Credulous* means tending to believe anything.

LAMENT
v. <luh-MENT>

_____

_____

_____

_____

LAMENT

to regret; to show grief for

Brett **lamented** the events of the day, he wished he had never won the ticket.

Cry Baby
despair, despondent, dour, lament, melancholy, morose

Word Alert: Something *lamentable* is something regrettable.

ENHANCE
v. <en-HANS>

_____

_____

_____

_____

ENHANCE

to make greater or better

Brett thinks that the feather **enhances** Katie's beauty, making her prettier than she already is.

HOMOGENEOUS
adj. <ho-mo-GEE-nee-yus>

_____

_____

_____

_____

HOMOGENEOUS

all of the same or similar kind

Brett and Katie are stuck in a **homogeneous** setting; there is nothing but sand in every direction.

Word Alert: If the prefix *hetero-* means *different*, what would *heterogeneous* mean?

SUPPRESS
v. <suh-PRES>

_____

_____

_____

_____

SUPPRESS

to put down; to hold back

Brett tried to **suppress** the pain he was feeling, but it was difficult to hold back.

Synonyms: quell, subdue

EXPEDITE
v. <EK-spi-dite>

_____

_____

_____

_____

EXPEDITE

to speed the progress of

Brett tried to **expedite** the digging, and his help allowed them to dig faster.

APPREHENSIVE
adj. <ap-ri-HEN-siv>

_____

_____

_____

_____

APPREHENSIVE

fearful

Brett became **apprehensive** upon seeing the frightening skull.

DEBUNK
v. <dih-BUHNK>

_____

_____

_____

_____

DEBUNK

to disprove or expose the falseness of

The glasses **debunked** Brett's idea that they had found the earliest form of human life.

Synonyms: refute, repudiate

LACONIC
adj. <luh-KON-ik>

_____

_____

_____

_____

LACONIC

using few words (often rudely or mysteriously)

Brett was **laconic**; he answered Katie's questions with only a few mysterious words.

Tight-Lipped
concise, laconic, reticent, succinct, terse

VULNERABLE
adj. <VUHL-ner-uh-buhl>

_____

_____

_____

_____

VULNERABLE

not protected against harm

Brett is **vulnerable** to the sun's rays; he gets sunburned easily.

Word Alert: If the prefix *in-* means not, what would *invulnerable* mean?

EXTOL
v. <ek-STOHL>

_____

_____

_____

_____

EXTOL

to praise

René **extolled** Brett's physical appearance, complimenting him on his good looks.

Hip Hip Hooray!
acclaim, adulation, commend, exalt, extol, laud

ELUCIDATE
v. <ih-LOO-si-dayt>

_____

_____

_____

_____

ELUCIDATE

to make clear

Brett attempts to **elucidate** the origin of the painting, telling a story to explain where it came from.

Word Alert: To elucidate something is to make it *lucid.*

NEBULOUS
adj. <NEB-yuh-luhs>

_____

_____

_____

_____

NEBULOUS

hazy, vague, or confused

How the painting got on the island remained **nebulous**, Brett and Katie still don't know why it's buried in the sand.

What the—?
abstruse, ambiguous, amorphous, enigmatic, equivocal, esoteric, nebulous

---

EULOGY
n. <YOO-luh-jee>

_____

_____

_____

_____

EULOGY

a written or spoken tribute (usually for someone who has died)

Katie delivers a **eulogy**, giving a speech in praise of the unknown dead man.

Word Alert: The prefix *eu-* means good, so eulogy literally means *good words.*

SOLEMN
adj. <SOL-uhm>

_____

_____

_____

_____

SOLEMN

serious and sober

Katie is **solemn** out of respect for the dead.

Serious Business
earnest, solemn, somber

FEASIBLE
adj. <FEE-zuh-buhl>

_____

_____

_____

_____

FEASIBLE

possible, workable, practical

Brett and Katie's idea is **feasible**: it might actually work.

EXUBERANT
adj. <ig-ZOO-ber-uhnt>

_____

_____

_____

_____

EXUBERANT

lively

Brett and Katie became **exuberant** when they saw the first flame appear on the picture and cheerfully danced around.

Party Hearty!
ebullient, exuberant, vivacious

IMAGINARY LARRY

David is preparing the perfect anniversary surprise for his girlfriend Shannon when an old friend from childhood arrives unannounced and the evening quickly spirals out of control.

AMBIGUOUS	unclear
SCRUPULOUS	thorough and careful
ADORN	to decorate
CAMARADERIE	goodwill among friends
SPECIOUS	seemingly true but actually logically false
REFUTE	to prove to be false
DELETERIOUS	harmful
HEED	to pay close attention to
ORTHODOX	commonly accepted; traditional
CONSTRUE	to interpret
ELATED	filled with delight
SCORN	intense hatred or disrespect
TEMPER	to soften or moderate
FLORID	elaborately or excessively ornamented; flowery
GARRULOUS	talkative
THWART	to stop or prevent
APPEASE	to bring peace, quiet, or calm to
ENCOMPASS	to include, to contain
CARNIVOROUS	meat-eating
ADVOCATE	to speak in favor of, promote
NEGLIGIBLE	insignificant; really small
GRATE	to irritate
BOLSTER	to support; to reinforce
DISCERN	to detect or perceive
FACILE	simple; easy
OBTRUSIVE	sticking out, noticeable; brash, meddling
INGENUOUS	innocent; honest and straightforward
DISCRETE	separate; distinct
REPUDIATE	to reject the validity of
INVOKE	to enforce or put into operation

AMBIGUOUS
adj. <am-BIG-yoo-uhs>

_____

_____

_____

_____

AMBIGUOUS

unclear

It was not clear why Shannon needed ski goggles and a wetsuit;
David's plans were extremely **ambiguous**.

What the—?
abstruse, ambiguous, amorphous, enigmatic, equivocal, esoteric,
nebulous

SCRUPULOUS
adj. <SKROO-pyuh-luhs>

_____

_____

_____

_____

SCRUPULOUS

thorough and careful

David **scrupulously** prepared his apartment for the big night,
thoroughly and carefully attending to every detail.

Synonyms: conscientious, meticulous

ADORN
v. <uh-DORN>

_____

_____

_____

_____

ADORN

to decorate

David **adorned** his apartment with rose petals, hoping Shannon
would be impressed with his decorations.

Synonyms: embellish

CAMARADERIE
n. <com-RAH-der-ee>

_____

_____

_____

_____

CAMARADERIE

goodwill among friends

Larry may be an imaginary friend, but the **camaraderie** he has
with David is real: they have a great time together.

BFF
amiable, affable, amicable, camaraderie, cordial, genial

SPECIOUS
adj. <SPEE-shus>

_____

_____

_____

_____

SPECIOUS

seemingly true but actually logically false

At first, Larry's argument seemed reasonable, but David quickly
realized it was **specious** and couldn't possibly be true.

Synonyms: spurious

REFUTE
v. <reh-FYOOT>

_____

_____

_____

REFUTE

to prove to be false

Larry insisted that David's girlfriend must be imaginary, but David **refuted** the accusation by showing him a very real photo.

Synonyms: debunk, repudiate

DELETERIOUS
adj. <del-uh-TEER-ee-us>

_____

_____

_____

DELETERIOUS

harmful

Eating a soup with Larry's ingredients would be **deleterious** to your health; it might just kill you.

Killer
bane, deleterious, pernicious

HEED
v. <HEED>

_____

_____

_____

HEED

to pay close attention to

David **heeds** the instructions in the cookbook and closely follows each step of the recipe.

ORTHODOX
adj. <OR-thuh-doks>

_____

_____

_____

ORTHODOX

commonly accepted; traditional

David opted not to wear a rambo outfit for his romantic dinner, and instead chose to follow Frankie's 10 commandments, wearing the more traditional, and **orthodox**, suit and tie.

CONSTRUE
v. <kuhn-STROO>

_____

_____

_____

_____

CONSTRUE

to interpret

After attempting to interpret the significance of each item, Shannon eventually **construed** them to mean that David is a spy.

If the prefix, mis- means wrong or bad, what would misconstrue mean?

ELATED
adj. <ih-LAYT-ed>

_____

_____

_____

_____

ELATED

filled with delight

Letting out a cry of delight, Shannon was obviously **elated** by David's surprise anniversary dinner.

Happy Camper
buoyant, ecstasy, elated, euphoria, felicity, mirth, sanguine

SCORN
n. <rhymes with *horn*>

_____

_____

_____

_____

SCORN

intense hatred or disrespect

Overcome by **scorn** for David, Shannon angrily insulted him.

Bad Blood
abhor, acrimony, animosity, antagonistic, contempt, disdain, enmity, rancor, scorn

TEMPER
v. <TEM-per>

_____

_____

_____

_____

TEMPER

to soften or moderate

David was able to **temper** Shannon's anger by calming her with sweet words and white wine.

Feel Better
alleviate, mitigate, mollify, temper

Word Alert: Something that is *temperate* is soft or moderate. *Temperance* is moderation or self-control.

FLORID
adj. <FLOR-id>

_____

_____

_____

_____

FLORID

elaborately or excessively ornamented; flowery

Larry defended his flowery shirt in an elaborate, **florid** speech.

Flashy
flamboyant, florid, garish, ornate

GARRULOUS
adj. <GAR-uh-lus or GAR-yoo-lus>

_____

_____

_____

_____

GARRULOUS

talkative

Garrulous by nature, Shannon talks endlessly to everyone she is with.

Synonyms: verbose, voluble

THWART
v. <rhymes with *wart*>

_____

_____

_____

_____

THWART

to stop or prevent

Trying to put an end to the dinner, Larry did everything he could to **thwart** David's attempts to get the soup.

Road Block
hamper, hinder, impede, inhibit, thwart

APPEASE
v. <uh-PEEZ>

_____

_____

_____

_____

APPEASE

to bring peace, quiet, or calm to

In order to calm Larry down, David **appeased** him by inviting him to the table and serving him soup.

Synonyms: conciliate

ENCOMPASS
v. <en-KUHM-puhs>

_____

_____

_____

_____

ENCOMPASS

to include, to contain

The soup obviously **encompassed** many flavors, but including some plastic in the recipe was probably not a good idea.

CARNIVOROUS
adj. <kar-NIV-er-uhs>

_____

_____

_____

_____

CARNIVOROUS

meat-eating

Because Larry is **carnivorous**, he eats meat and could not stop himself from devouring all of the chicken.

ADVOCATE
v. <AD-vuh-kate>

_____

_____

_____

_____

ADVOCATE

to speak in favor of, promote

Larry strongly **advocated** the use of avocados; he offered many reasons for why they are the greatest "vegetable-fruit" on earth.

Synonyms: espouse

Word Alert: An *advocate* is a person who advocates. *Advocacy* is the act of advocating .

NEGLIGIBLE
adj. <NEG-li-juh-buhl>

_____

_____

_____

_____

NEGLIGIBLE

insignificant; really small

The plate had only a **negligible** amount of chicken, so little it was almost non-existent.

Synonyms: frivolous, inconsequential, trivial

GRATE
v. <rhymes with *late*>

_____

_____

_____

_____

GRATE

to irritate

Larry was so **grating** and annoying that David quickly became irritated and had to leave the table.

Synonyms: exasperate

BOLSTER
v. <BOHL-ster>

_____

_____

_____

_____

BOLSTER

to support; to reinforce

David **bolstered** his promise to Larry with a pinky swear. And then David **bolstered** the chair to keep Larry from escaping; both of these examples should really reinforce – and **bolster** – the definition of the word!

Synonyms: buttress

DISCERN
v. <di-SURN>

_____

_____

_____

_____

DISCERN

to detect or perceive

Shannon detected something strange about the evening and is able to **discern** that either David is hiding something or is losing his mind.

Eagle Eye
acuity, astute, discern, incisive, keen, perspicacity

Word Alert: To be discerning is to be insightful or perceptive.

FACILE
adj. <FASS-il>

_____

_____

_____

_____

FACILE

simple; easy

Larry made a **facile** escape, easily leaving the room by just opening the door.

Word Alert: To *facilitate* is to make something easier.

OBTRUSIVE
adj. <uhb-TROO-siv>

_____

_____

_____

_____

OBTRUSIVE

sticking out, noticeable; brash, meddling

Larry is **obtrusive** in everything he does, impossible to ignore and always getting in the way.

Synonyms: officious

Word Alert: To *obtrude* is to be obtrusive.

INGENUOUS
adj. <in-JEN-yoo-uhs>

_____

_____

_____

_____

INGENUOUS

innocent; honest and straightforward

Deciding it was time to be honest, David made an **ingenuous** confession about Imaginary Larry.

Synonyms: candid, forthright

Word Alert: If the prefix *dis-* means *not*, what would *disingenuous* mean?

DISCRETE
adj. <di-SKREET>

_____

_____

_____

_____

DISCRETE

separate; distinct

David offered to split his week into separate, **discrete** time slots for Shannon and Larry in order to divide his time between them.

Word Alert: Don't confuse this word with *discreet*.

REPUDIATE
v. <ri-PYOO-dee-ate>

_____

_____

_____

_____

_____

REPUDIATE

to reject the validity of

Shannon **repudiated** David's explanation of Larry by offering several reasons why his confession had to be false.

Synonyms: debunk, refute

INVOKE
v. <in-VOHK>

_____

_____

_____

_____

_____

INVOKE

to enforce or put into operation

David **invoked** the new calendar rule so he could be alone; with the rule in place, he was able to force Larry to leave.

Word Alert: An *invocation* is something that invokes something else.

IMAGINARY LARRY: THE FELLOWSHIP OF THE MEYERSON

David and Larry tell the story of Henry Meyerson and his wife Natalie. After she is kidnapped by a mysterious stranger, Henry sets off on a desperate quest to rescue her and recruits the help of some new friends along the way.

VAPID	lacking liveliness or interest; dull
AMELIORATE	to improve
ZEALOUS	filled with or motivated by enthusiastic devotion
UNASSUMING	not showy or arrogant; modest; plain
DIVISIVE	creating disagreement or dissent
MAGNANIMOUS	noble and generous in spirit
TREACHERY	deliberate betrayal of trust
SPURIOUS	not genuine; false
SCRUTINIZE	to examine carefully
LUCID	clear
ARID	dry
AMICABLE	friendly
INDIGENOUS	native
ESPOUSE	to give one's support to
INSULAR	isolated; narrow-minded
LAVISH	excessive; plentiful
CALLOUS	emotionally hardened or unfeeling
VIGILANT	alert; watchful
CIRCUITOUS	being or taking a roundabout course
DIGRESS	to stray from the main subject

VAPID
adj. <VAP-id>

_____

_____

_____

_____

VAPID

lacking liveliness or interest; dull

David's afternoon was **vapid**, playing war by himself was utterly boring and dull.

AMELIORATE
v. <uh-MEE-lee-uh-rayt>

_____

_____

_____

_____

AMELIORATE

to improve

In an effort to **ameliorate** his friend's frustration, Larry offered David his favorite toy to improve his mood.

ZEALOUS
adj. <ZELL-us>

_____

_____

_____

_____

ZEALOUS

filled with or motivated by enthusiastic devotion

Overcome by enthusiasm, Larry **zealously** tried to convince David to use his imagination.

X-treme Intensity!
ardor, fervent, galvanize, impassioned, zealous

Word Alert: A *zealot* is a zealous person. *Zeal* (rhymes with "seal") is enthusiasm.

UNASSUMING
adj. <un-uh-SOO-ming>

_____

_____

_____

_____

UNASSUMING

not showy or arrogant; modest; plain

Henry led a modest, **unassuming** life; his house, his job and his interests were all simple and plain.

DIVISIVE
adj. <di-VICE-iv>

_____

_____

_____

_____

DIVISIVE

creating disagreement or dissent

The issue of having children was a **divisive** one and Henry and Natalie fought about it constantly.

Synonyms: discordant [see discord]

Word Alert: Divisive comes from the same root as *divide*.

MAGNANIMOUS
adj. <mag-NAN-uh-muhs>

_____

_____

_____

_____

MAGNANIMOUS

noble and generous in spirit

Natalie generously offered the stranger money for food, a **magnanimous** gesture.

Synonyms: benevolent

TREACHERY
n. <TRECH-uh-ree>

_____

_____

_____

_____

TREACHERY

deliberate betrayal of trust

Betraying Natalie's trust, the mysterious stranger used **treachery** to kidnap her.

Shady
cunning, duplicity, guile, treachery

SPURIOUS
adj. <SPYOOR-ee-uhs>

_____

_____

_____

_____

SPURIOUS

not genuine; false

The note left for Henry was obviously **spurious**; it could not possibly have been genuine.

Synonyms: specious

SCRUTINIZE
v. <SKROOT-in-ize>

_____

_____

_____

_____

SCRUTINIZE

to examine carefully

Henry carefully examined the handwriting from two different notes, **scrutinizing** every detail for clues.

Word Alert: Scrutiny is the act of examining. Something *inscrutable* cannot be examined or understood.

LUCID
adj. <LOO-sid>

_____

_____

_____

_____

LUCID

clear

The bag provided Henry with a **lucid** picture of what happened to Natalie, making it very clear she had been kidnapped.

Word Alert: To *elucidate* is to make something lucid.

ARID
adj. <A-rid>

_____

_____

_____

_____

ARID

dry

Henry walked through the **arid** desert, eventually collapsing from the effects of the hot and dry climate.

AMICABLE
adj. <AM-ih-kuh-buhl>

_____

_____

_____

_____

AMICABLE

friendly

Henry is discovered by an **amicable** creature named Crabby Cakes who kindly offers him bread and water.

BFF
amiable, affable, amicable, camaraderie, cordial, genial

INDIGENOUS
adj. <in-DIH-jen-us>

_____

_____

_____

_____

INDIGENOUS

native

The Shell-ites, the Albino Hogs and the mini Koala are **indigenous** species, having lived in the desert for thousands of years.

ESPOUSE
v. <ih-SPOUZ>

_____

_____

_____

_____

ESPOUSE

to give one's support to

After hearing Henry's story, Crabby Cakes decides to **espouse** Henry's cause and declares his support for the quest.

Synonyms: advocate

INSULAR
adj. <IN-syu-ler>

_____

_____

_____

_____

INSULAR

isolated; narrow-minded

Insular in his beliefs, the narrow-minded King believes the world is flat and brides should be kidnapped.

Synonyms: provincial

LAVISH
adj. <LAV-ish>

_____

_____

_____

_____

CALLOUS
adj. <KAL-uhs>

_____

_____

_____

_____

VIGILANT
adj. <VIJ-uh-luhnt>

_____

_____

_____

_____

CIRCUITOUS
adj. <sur-KYOO-ih-tus>

_____

_____

_____

_____

DIGRESS
v. <di-GRES>

_____

_____

_____

_____

LAVISH

excessive; plentiful

Trying to impress Natalie with **lavish** gifts, the King presents her with an abundance of riches.

Overboard
exorbitant, extravagant, lavish, luxurious, opulent

CALLOUS

emotionally hardened or unfeeling

The King was unaffected by Natalie's emotional pleas and **callously** dismissed her tears.

VIGILANT

alert; watchful

Unblinking and watchful, the Eye remained **vigilant** as Henry and Crabby Cakes approached.

Synonyms: wary

CIRCUITOUS

being or taking a roundabout course

To avoid danger, Henry and Crabby Cakes took a **circuitous** route, winding their way through the mountains.

DIGRESS

to stray from the main subject

Larry **digressed**, straying from the story to describe how hungry he was rather than focusing on the main idea of the adventure.

Word Alert: A *digression* is an act of digressing.

IMAGINARY LARRY: THE BATTLE FOR DESERT MALAGUAY

We rejoin Henry and Crabby Cakes as they take on the King's fearsome guards and try to save Natalie before she is lost forever.

AMENABLE	open to advice or suggestion
ORNATE	excessively decorated
VILIFY	to say bad things about, to make into a villain
EXTRAVAGANT	excessive
INSTIGATE	to stir up
BELLIGERENT	eager to fight
EVOKE	to summon or call forth
COHESIVE	sticking or holding together
ENTRENCH	to fix firmly or securely
PRAGMATIC	practical
DISSENT	disagreement
ALIENATE	to make unfriendly or hostile
CONSENSUS	general agreement
DENOUNCE	to condemn openly
RELINQUISH	to give up; to release
SUBVERT	to ruin; to overthrow
CONSTITUENT	a component
BURGEON	to grow
PROSPERITY	success; being well-off
HACKNEYED	overused

AMENABLE
adj. <uh-MEN-uh-buhl>

_____
_____
_____
_____

AMENABLE

open to advice or suggestion

Much to David's surprise, Larry is **amenable** and completely open to his suggestions.

ORNATE
adj. <or-NAYT>

_____
_____
_____
_____

ORNATE

excessively decorated

The dress was incredibly **ornate** and its elaborate decorations.seemed almost excessive.

Flashy
flamboyant, florid, garish, ornate

VILIFY
v. <VIL-uh-fahy>

_____
_____
_____
_____

VILIFY

to say bad things about, to make into a villain

Natalie attacks the King with a long list of insults, **vilifying** him for his actions.

Trash Talk
belittle, decry, denigrate, denounce, deprecate, deride, disparage, vilify

---

EXTRAVAGANT
adj. <ek-STRAV-uh-guhnt>

_____
_____
_____
_____

EXTRAVAGANT

excessive

A massive structure with 50 bedrooms and its own zipcode, the castle was **extravagant** in every way.

Overboard
exorbitant, extravagant, lavish, luxurious, opulent

INSTIGATE
v. <IN-sti-gate>

_____
_____
_____
_____
_____

INSTIGATE

to stir up

Henry **instigated** the King's anger, provoking him with a series of offensive comments.

Synonyms: provoke [see provocative]

BELLIGERENT
adj. <buh-LIH-jer-uhnt>

_____

_____

_____

_____

BELLIGERENT

eager to fight

The King is **belligerent**, eager to fight anyone who angers him.

Fight Club
belligerent, cantankerous, contend, irate, pugnacious

Word Alert: The *belli-* root means *combat.* So *bellicose* means *hostile or warlike.*

EVOKE
v. <ih-VOHK>

_____

_____

_____

_____

EVOKE

to summon or call forth

Summoning the Skelosauruses, the King **evoked** the power of the mythical beasts to intimidate Henry.

COHESIVE
adj. <koh-HEE-siv>

_____

_____

_____

_____

COHESIVE

sticking or holding together

Crabby Cakes and Henry remained a **cohesive** team even when danger threatened to rip them apart.

Word Alert: To *cohere* means to stick together. *Coherent* comes from the same root.

ENTRENCH
v. <en-TRENCH>

_____

_____

_____

_____

ENTRENCH

to fix firmly or securely

Crabby Cakes refused to change his mind about using violence; his beliefs remained firmly **entrenched**.

PRAGMATIC
adj. <prag-MAT-ik>

_____

_____

_____

_____

PRAGMATIC

practical

Crabby Cakes is **pragmatic** in his approach to stopping the fearsome Skelosauruses, his practical solution is to quickly build a defensive wall out of the wet sand.

Synonyms: utilitarian

DISSENT
n. <di-SENT>

_____

_____

_____

_____

DISSENT

disagreement

As the creatures disagree, it is obvious there is **dissent** within the group.

Word Alert: Dissent can also be a verb meaning *to disagree.*

ALIENATE
v. <AY-lee-uh-nayt>

_____

_____

_____

_____

ALIENATE

to make unfriendly or hostile

When the King's insults **alienated** the Skelosauruses, they quickly become hostile towards him.

Synonyms: estrange

CONSENSUS
n. <kuhn-SEN-suhs>

_____

_____

_____

_____

CONSENSUS

general agreement

There is a **consensus**, a general agreement, that the King has gone too far.

Like-Minded
accord, concord, concur, conform, consensus, uniform

DENOUNCE
v. <di-NOUNS>

_____

_____

_____

_____

DENOUNCE

to condemn openly

The King is **denounced** by his subjects as they openly criticize him.

Trash Talk
belittle, decry, denigrate, denounce, deprecate, deride, disparage, vilify

RELINQUISH
v. <ri-LIN-kwish>

_____

_____

_____

_____

RELINQUISH

to give up; to release

Realizing his defeat, the King **relinquishes** Natalie, releasing her from captivity.

Synonyms: renounce

SUBVERT

v. <suhb-VURT>

_____

_____

_____

_____

SUBVERT

to ruin; to overthrow

The dragon is able to **subvert** the rule of the King, overthrowing him and ending his tyranny.

Word Alert: Something *subversive* is intended or serving to subvert.

CONSTITUENT

n. <kuhn-STITCH-oo-uhnt>

_____

_____

_____

_____

CONSTITUENT

a component

Henry identified the **constituent** missing from the soil for all of these years, the one component necessary to make things grow in the desert.

Word Alert: To *constitute* something is to be a constituent of it.

BURGEON

v. <BUR-juhn>

_____

_____

_____

_____

BURGEON

to grow

The fertilizer helped the plants to **burgeon** rapidly, turning the sand into a lush paradise in just a few weeks.

Synonyms: flourish

PROSPERITY

n. <pro-SPER-i-tee>

_____

_____

_____

_____

PROSPERITY

success; being well-off

A hero, Henry enjoyed a life of wealth and **prosperity** after he introduced fertilizer to the desert.

Word Alert: To *prosper* is to be *prosperous* and possess prosperity.

HACKNEYED

adj. <HACK-need>

_____

_____

_____

_____

HACKNEYED

overused

David's **hackneyed** ending to the story was completely unoriginal; in fact, "they lived happily ever after" is probably the most overused ending to a fairly tale in history.

Played Out
banal, hackneyed, insipid, mundane, prosaic, trite

MAD SCIENTISTS PART 1

Tired of their dull laboratory work, Dr. Perkins and her assistant Christina decide to invent something truly remarkable.

DISGRUNTLED	unhappy
PROLIFIC	producing abundant works or results
REVERE	to respect, honor or admire
RESOLUTE	firm or determined
AUSPICIOUS	favorable; successful
MERCURIAL	changeable, erratic
PROSAIC	lacking in imagination; dull
SMUG	self-satisfied (especially in a mocking way)
NOVEL	strikingly new or different
EBULLIENT	enthusiastic, lively
OBDURATE	stubbornly persistent in wrongdoing
FOSTER	to promote the development of
EXACTING	requiring great care or effort
DIMINUTIVE	tiny
ERUDITE	scholarly, well educated
ANECDOTE	a short account of an interesting or humorous incident
AUDACITY	disrespectful boldness
IMPUGN	to attack as false or wrong, to challenge or question
HINDER	to be or get in the way of
SHREWD	smart in a sneaky or tricky manner

DISGRUNTLED
adj. <dis-GRUHN-tuld>

_____

_____

_____

_____

DISGRUNTLED

unhappy

Dr. Perkins is **disgruntled** with her job, unhappy that she is not contributing more to society.

PROLIFIC
adj. <pruh-LIF-ik>

_____

_____

_____

_____

PROLIFIC

producing abundant works or results

Dr. Perkins has had a **prolific** career, inventing many amazing things like fake snow, the seedless watermelon, and hair gel.

REVERE
v. <ri-VEER>

_____

_____

_____

_____

REVERE

to respect, honor or admire

Dr. Perkins **reveres** her hero Alexander Graham Bell; she has great respect for his scientific achievements.

Synonyms: esteem

Word Alert: *Reverence* is the act of revering.
Word Alert: If the prefix, *ir-* means *not*, what would *irreverent* mean?

RESOLUTE
adj. <REZ-uh-loot>

_____

_____

_____

_____

RESOLUTE

firm or determined

Determined to make a giant contribution to the world, Dr. Perkins is **resolute** in her desire to invent something revolutionary.

Synonyms: steadfast

AUSPICIOUS
adj. <aw-SPISH-uhs>

_____

_____

_____

_____

AUSPICIOUS

favorable; successful

Christina received an **auspicious** text; her horoscope predicted that the invention would be successful.

Word Alert: An *auspice* is auspicious sign.

MERCURIAL
adj. <mer-KYOOR-ee-uhl>

_____

_____

_____

_____

PROSAIC
adj. <pro-ZAY-ic>

_____

_____

_____

_____

SMUG
adj. <rhymes with *bug*>

_____

_____

_____

_____

NOVEL
adj. <NOV-uhl>

_____

_____

_____

_____

EBULLIENT
adj. <eh-BOO-lee-ent>

_____

_____

_____

_____

MERCURIAL

changeable, erratic

Her expressions changing wildly from despair to joy, Christina was **mercurial** while she brainstormed.

Unpredictable
arbitrary, capricious, erratic, impetuous, mercurial, mutable, volatile, whimsical

PROSAIC

lacking in imagination; dull

Christina's **prosaic** idea for the seedless cantaloupe was unoriginal and boring.

Played Out
banal, hackneyed, insipid, mundane, prosaic, trite

SMUG

self-satisfied (especially in a mocking way)

Excessively proud of her new idea, Dr. Perkins **smugly** described herself as brilliant.

Synonyms: complacent

NOVEL

strikingly new or different

The invention of book pills was certainly a **novel** one – no one had ever come up with anything like it before.

Synonyms: innovative

Word Alert: Novel and *innovative* come from the same root.

EBULLIENT

enthusiastic, lively

Dr. Perkins and Christina were **ebullient**, enthusiastically celebrating and dancing in the laboratory.

Party Hearty!
ebullient, exuberant, vivacious

OBDURATE
adj. <OB-doo-rit>

_____

_____

_____

_____

FOSTER
v. <FAW-ster>

_____

_____

_____

_____

EXACTING
adj. <eg-ZAK-ting>

_____

_____

_____

_____

DIMINUTIVE
adj. <di-MIN-yuh-tiv>

_____

_____

_____

_____

ERUDITE
adj. <ER-yoo-dite>

_____

_____

_____

_____

OBDURATE

stubbornly persistent in wrongdoing

Even after repeated warnings to stop, Christina was **obdurate**, stubbornly continuing to mix the chemicals.

Pig-Headed
dogged, dogmatic, intransigent, obdurate, obstinate, tenacity

FOSTER

to promote the development of

Dr. Perkins **fostered** Christina's understanding of chemistry; she explained each aspect of the experiment to help Christina become a better scientist.

Synonyms: nurture

EXACTING

requiring great care or effort

Dr. Perkins' directions to Christina were **exacting**, and so required Christina to take great care during the experiment.

DIMINUTIVE

tiny

The pill was **diminutive**: an entire book was contained in one tiny capsule.

Word Alert: Something *diminutive* is very small.

ERUDITE

scholarly, well educated

After taking the pills, Christina became **erudite**; suddenly she was well educated and even able to quote Thoreau.

Word Alert: *Erudition* means knowledge or learning.

ANECDOTE
n. <AN-ik-doht>

_____

_____

_____

_____

ANECDOTE

a short account of an interesting or humorous incident

Dr. Perkins tells an **anecdote** about her former assistant, and in this brief and amusing account she warns Christina of the dangers of taking more pills.

AUDACITY
n. <aw-DAS-i-tee>

_____

_____

_____

_____

AUDACITY

disrespectful boldness

Despite Dr. Perkins' commands to stop taking the pills, Christina had the **audacity** to take one anyway, showing disrespectful boldness to her superior.

Synonyms: insolence [see insolent]

Word Alert: Someone *audacious* acts with audacity.

IMPUGN
v. <im-PYOON>

_____

_____

_____

_____

IMPUGN

to attack as false or wrong, to challenge or question

Christina **impugned** Dr. Perkins' expertise, challenging her qualifications to run the lab.

HINDER
v. <HIN-der>

_____

_____

_____

_____

HINDER

to be or get in the way of

Dr. Perkins reached for the pills, but Christina **hindered** her movements, blocking any attempt to grab the capsules.

Road Block
hamper, hinder, impede, inhibit, thwart

Word Alert: A *hindrance* is something that hinders.

SHREWD
adj. <SHROOD>

_____

_____

_____

_____

SHREWD

smart in a sneaky or tricky manner

Shrewdly offering Christina a special pill, Dr. Perkins cleverly tricked her assistant into taking something that actually made her dumber.

Wise Guy
circumspect, discreet, judicious, prudent, sagacious, shrewd

MAD SCIENTISTS PART 2

A celebrity approaches Dr. Perkins and Christina looking to get an edge in competition and poses a moral dilemma to the scientists.

INTELLIGIBLE	capable of being understood
ALACRITY	eagerness, enthusiasm
BRUSQUE	rudely brief
SPURN	to reject with disrespect
PUGNACIOUS	eager to fight
FORTHRIGHT	honest, direct, straightforward
CONJECTURE	guesswork
PERVASIVE	spread throughout
DEMEAN	to lower in status or worth
DIFFIDENCE	a lack of self-confidence, shyness
CONTRITE	feeling or expressing remorse
EFFUSIVE	overflowing (usually referring to emotions)
TRANSITORY	existing only briefly
DECORUM	correct or appropriate behavior
ILLICIT	not permitted by custom or law
BOMBASTIC	using arrogant or pretentious speech
DISCREET	careful in one's conduct or speech
ERRATIC	irregular
IMPERIOUS	arrogantly authoritative or overbearing
DOCILE	easily managed or taught

INTELLIGIBLE
adj. <in-TEL-i-juh-buhl>

_____

_____

_____

_____

INTELLIGIBLE

capable of being understood

Without a thick Italian accent, Natalio's speech became **intelligible** and Christina could easily understand him.

Word Alert: If the prefix *un-* means *not*, what would *unintelligible* mean?

ALACRITY
n. <uh-LAK-ri-tee>

_____

_____

_____

_____

ALACRITY

eagerness, enthusiasm

Christina accepted Natalio's offer with **alacrity**; when she discovered he would pay her salary for the rest of her life she was filled with enthusiasm.

BRUSQUE
adj. <rhymes with *tusk*>

_____

_____

_____

_____

BRUSQUE

rudely brief

Dr. Perkins' response to Christina was **brusque**, as she dismissed the request quickly and rudely.

SPURN
v. <rhymes with *burn*>

_____

_____

_____

_____

SPURN

to reject with disrespect

Spurning Christina's unethical proposition, Dr. Perkins rejected it without any consideration.

PUGNACIOUS
adj. <puhg-NAY-shuhs>

_____

_____

_____

_____

PUGNACIOUS

eager to fight

Eager to fight, a **pugnacious** Christina is ready to brawl with Dr. Perkins to get her way.

Fight Club
belligerent, cantankerous, contend, irate, pugnacious

FORTHRIGHT
adj. <FORTH-rite>

_____

_____

_____

_____

FORTHRIGHT

honest, direct, straightforward

Dr. Perkins is **forthright** and honest when telling Christina about the risk involved in creating the drug.

Synonyms: ingenuous, candid

CONJECTURE
n. <kuhn-JEK-cher>

_____

_____

_____

_____

CONJECTURE

guesswork

Dr. Perkins dismisses Christina's formula as pure **conjecture**; it was merely guesswork.

PERVASIVE
adj. <per-VAY-siv>

_____

_____

_____

_____

PERVASIVE

spread throughout

The terrible smell of the mixture was **pervasive** and spread throughout the entire lab.

Word Alert: To *pervade* is to be pervasive.

DEMEAN
v. <di-MEEN>

_____

_____

_____

_____

DEMEAN

to lower in status or worth

Dr. Perkins was **demeaning** to Christina, putting her down and claiming she could not do anything right.

DIFFIDENCE
n. <DIF-ih-duhns>

_____

_____

_____

_____

DIFFIDENCE

a lack of self-confidence, shyness

Christina suddenly became **diffident** as the criticism left her shy and lacking self-confidence.

CONTRITE
adj. <kon-TRITE>

_____

_____

_____

_____

CONTRITE

feeling or expressing remorse

Because she felt sorry for what she said, Dr. Perkins was **contrite** and apologized to Christina.

Synonyms: penitent

EFFUSIVE
adj. <ih-FYOO-siv>

_____

_____

_____

_____

EFFUSIVE

overflowing (usually referring to emotions)

Effusively happy, Christina seemed to overflow with excitement.

TRANSITORY
adj. <TRAN-si-tor-ee>

_____

_____

_____

_____

TRANSITORY

existing only briefly

The effects of the Pure Speed pills were **transitory**, lasting only a few seconds.

Gone with the Wind
elusive, ephemeral, evanescent, evasive, transient, transitory

---

DECORUM
n. <di-KOHR-uhm>

_____

_____

_____

_____

DECORUM

correct or appropriate behavior

Dr. Perkins attempted to show Christina how to act with **decorum**, teaching her how to curtsy and display proper manners.

Word Alert: To be *decorous* is to act with decorum.

ILLICIT
adj. <ih-LIS-it>

_____

_____

_____

_____

ILLICIT

not permitted by custom or law

Dr. Perkins and Christina broke the law by making an **illicit** performance enhancing drug.

Word Alert: Don't confuse this word with *elicit*, which means *to evoke*.

BOMBASTIC
adj. <bom-BAS-tik>

_____

_____

_____

_____

BOMBASTIC

using arrogant or pretentious speech

Natalio's **bombastic** talk left Perkins and Christina disgusted, as he arrogantly claimed to be the richest, smartest and soon-to-be fastest person he knows.

Cocky
bombastic, condescend, grandiose, haughty, patronize, pompous, pretentious

Word Alert: Bombastic is also close in meaning to *verbose*.

DISCREET
adj. <di-SKREET>

_____

_____

_____

_____

DISCREET

careful in one's conduct or speech

Dr. Perkins **discreetly** switches the pills, careful not to let Natalio see what she's doing

Wise Guy
circumspect, discreet, judicious, prudent, sagacious, shrewd

Word Alert: Discretion is the quality of being discreet.
Word Alert: Don't confuse this word with *discrete*.

ERRATIC
adj. <ih-RAT-ik>

_____

_____

_____

_____

ERRATIC

irregular

After Dr. Perkins secretly switched the pills, the pitch of Belastracci's voice fluctuated **erratically** from high to low.

Unpredictable
arbitrary, capricious, erratic, impetuous, mercurial, mutable, volatile, whimsical

---

IMPERIOUS
adj. <im-PEER-ee-uhs>

_____

_____

_____

_____

IMPERIOUS

arrogantly authoritative or overbearing

Natalio's **imperious** demands for the pills seemed even more authoritative and commanding because of his exceptionally deep voice.

DOCILE
adj. <DOSS-uhl>

_____

_____

_____

_____

DOCILE

easily managed or taught

Desperate for the pills, Natalio quickly became **docile** and was willing to do anything Perkins and Christina commanded to get his hands on the Pure Speed.

Synonyms: tractable

SPEEDWALKERS: THE LEGEND OF MAX WIND

Legendary speedwalker Max Wind must battle his demons and come out of retirement for one last race against the world champion Natalio Belastracci.

CHRONIC	continuing or lingering
DERIDE	to speak of or treat with cruelty
IMPEDE	to be or get in the way of
POMPOUS	exaggeratedly self-important
CONTEMPT	a lack of respect and intense dislike
BRAZEN	rudely bold
PERSPICACITY	a high level of perception or understanding
JADED	weary, worn out
SUCCINCT	precise expression using few words
MOLLIFY	to soften, to ease the anger of
INVIGORATE	to give life or energy to
DIVULGE	to make known, reveal
FRIVOLOUS	unworthy of serious attention
CATHARTIC	emotionally cleansing or relieving
DOGGED	stubbornly persevering
ENERVATE	to weaken or drain of energy
DOUR	gloomy
FLAGRANT	obviously bad or offensive
VICARIOUS	felt or undergone as if one were taking part in the experience or feelings of another
EUPHORIA	a feeling of great happiness

CHRONIC
adj. <KRON-ic>

_____

_____

_____

_____

CHRONIC

continuing or lingering

Max Wind has **chronic** nightmares; he has a recurring dream that keeps him awake every night.

DERIDE
v. <di-RIDE>

_____

_____

_____

_____

DERIDE

to speak of or treat with cruelty

The psychiatrist **derided** Max's issues, cruelly making fun of his mental state.

Trash Talk
belittle, decry, denigrate, denounce, deprecate, deride, disparage, vilify

Word Alert: *Derision* is the act of deriding. To be *derisive* is to act with derision.

IMPEDE
v. <im-PEED>

_____

_____

_____

_____

IMPEDE

to be or get in the way of

Max **impeded** the runner's movement, repeatedly getting in his way.

Road Block
hamper, hinder, impede, inhibit, thwart

Word Alert: An *impediment* is something that impedes.

POMPOUS
adj. <POM-puhs>

_____

_____

_____

_____

POMPOUS

exaggeratedly self-important

Natalio is incredibly **pompous**: he thinks he is the greatest speedwalker in the world.

Cocky
bombastic, condescend, grandiose, haughty, patronize, pompous, pretentious

---

CONTEMPT
n. <kuhn-TEMPT>

_____

_____

_____

_____

CONTEMPT

a lack of respect and intense dislike

Natalio has **contempt** for Max Wind; he hates him.

Bad Blood
abhor, acrimony, animosity, antagonistic, contempt, disdain, enmity, rancor, scorn

Word Alert: Someone *contemptuous* is full of contempt. Something *contemptible* is worthy of contempt.

BRAZEN
adj. <BRAY-zuhn>

_____

_____

_____

_____

BRAZEN

rudely bold

Natalio sent a **brazen** letter; first insulting Max and then boldly challenging him to a race.

PERSPICACITY
n. <pur-spi-KAS-i-tee>

_____

_____

_____

_____

PERSPICACITY

a high level of perception or understanding

Frankie demonstrated his **perspicacity** by instantly perceiving Max had not been training for the race.

Eagle Eye
acuity, astute, discern, incisive, keen, perspicacity

Word Alert: A *perspicacious* person possesses perspicacity.

JADED
adj. <JAY-ded>

_____

_____

_____

_____

JADED

weary, worn out

Max is **jaded**, completely worn out by his experiences.

SUCCINCT
adj. <suk-SINKT or suh-SINKT>

_____

_____

_____

_____

SUCCINCT

precise expression using few words

The sportscaster was **succinct** when he described Max in just one word: Chicken.

Tight-Lipped
concise, laconic, reticent, succinct, terse

MOLLIFY
v. <MOL-uh-fye>

_____

_____

_____

_____

_____

MOLLIFY

to soften, to ease the anger of

Bruno's compliment **mollifies** Natalio, easing his anger and making him smile.

Feel Better
alleviate, mitigate, mollify, temper

INVIGORATE
v. <in-VIG-uh-rayt>

_____

_____

_____

_____

INVIGORATE

to give life or energy to

Max was **invigorated** by Frankie's inspirational speech, leaping off the bleachers with new life.

DIVULGE
v. <di-VUHLJ>

_____

_____

_____

_____

DIVULGE

to make known, reveal

Max **divulged** his terrible secret, revealing that since the accident he cannot swing his arms when he walks.

FRIVOLOUS
adj. <FRIV-uh-luhs>

_____

_____

_____

_____

FRIVOLOUS

unworthy of serious attention

Natalio thinks that training is **frivolous**, he does not need to spend serious time preparing for his race with Max.

Synonyms: inconsequential, negligible, trivial

Word Alert: A *frivolity* is something that is frivolous.

CATHARTIC
adj. <kuh-THAR-tik>

_____

_____

_____

_____

CATHARTIC

emotionally cleansing or relieving

When Max broke down and cried, it was a **cathartic** moment that unleashed his emotions.

DOGGED
adj. <DOG-ed>

_____

_____

_____

_____

DOGGED

stubbornly persevering

Max showed **dogged** perseverance, training and training but never giving up.

Pig-Headed
dogged, dogmatic, intransigent, obdurate, obstinate, tenacity

ENERVATE
v. <EN-er-vayt>

_____

_____

_____

_____

ENERVATE

to weaken or drain of energy

The training **enervated** Frankie and by the end of the day he collapsed.

Synonyms: debilitate

DOUR
adj. <rhymes with *hour*>

_____

_____

_____

_____

DOUR

gloomy

The mood in the hospital room was **dour**; Max was saddened by Frankie's poor health.

Cry Baby
despair, despondent, dour, lament, melancholy, morose

FLAGRANT
adj. <FLAY-gruhnt>

_____

_____

_____

_____

FLAGRANT

obviously bad or offensive

Natalio **flagrantly** cheats, obviously taking illegal pills to try to win the race.

VICARIOUS
adj. <vye-CAIR-ee-us>

_____

_____

_____

_____

VICARIOUS

felt or undergone as if one were taking part in the experience or feelings of another

Frankie **vicariously** experiences the race, moving his arms and feeling like he is the one racing.

EUPHORIA
n. <yoo-FOR-ee-a>

_____

_____

_____

_____

EUPHORIA

a feeling of great happiness

Max and Frankie are overcome with **euphoria**, enthusiastically celebrating the victory as the crowd goes wild.

Happy Camper
buoyant, ecstasy, elated, euphoria, felicity, mirth, sanguine

Word Alert: To be *euphoric* is to feel euphoria.

SPEEDWALKERS: THE RISE AND FALL OF RENÉ DUPONT

René Dupont, the artist, discovers his natural talent for speedwalking. He must battle not only the mysterious Bird of Prey but also his love of money.

APATHETIC	lacking interest, concern, or emotion
ENUMERATE	to specify individually; to count
RESILIENT	able to recover promptly
EXEMPLARY	worthy of imitation
IMPETUOUS	impulsive, unthinking
OPULENT	rich and superior in quality
WARY	on guard, cautious, watchful
COMPLACENT	self-satisfied to the point of inactivity; unconcerned
IDIOSYNCRATIC	peculiar to an individual
CORDIAL	friendly, warm, polite
CANTANKEROUS	ill-tempered
AVARICE	greed
DECRY	to condemn openly
PRECIPITOUS	extremely steep
BENEVOLENT	inclined to perform kind acts
DISDAIN	intense dislike
INSOLENT	disrespectfully arrogant
GRATUITOUS	unnecessary
STEADFAST	firm and dependable
SOMBER	gloomy

APATHETIC

adj. <ap-uh-THET-ik>

_____

_____

_____

_____

APATHETIC

lacking interest, concern, or emotion

René was **apathetic** in responding to Darlene's questions; he didn't seem interested in anything she said.

Synonyms: indifferent, nonchalant

Word Alert: *Apathy* is an apathetic state of mind.

ENUMERATE

v. <i-NOO-muh-rayt>

_____

_____

_____

_____

ENUMERATE

to specify individually; to count

René **enumerated** his talents, listing individually each of his skills.

RESILIENT

adj. <ri-ZIL-yuhnt>

_____

_____

_____

_____

RESILIENT

able to recover promptly

After falling down early in the race, René was **resilient**, quickly recovering in order to win.

EXEMPLARY

adj. <ig-ZEM-pluh-ree>

_____

_____

_____

_____

EXEMPLARY

worthy of imitation

René thinks the sportscaster is **exemplary** and tries to imitate him during the interview.

Word Alert: An *exemplar* is a person who is worthy of imitation.

IMPETUOUS

adj. <im-PET-choo-uhs>

_____

_____

_____

_____

IMPETUOUS

impulsive, unthinking

Without much thought and acting on impulse, René **impetuously** asked Darlene to marry him.

Unpredictable
arbitrary, capricious, erratic, impetuous, mercurial, mutable, volatile, whimsical

OPULENT
adj. <OP-yuh-luhnt>

_____

_____

_____

WARY
adj. <WAIR-ee (rhymes with *hairy*)>

_____

_____

_____

COMPLACENT
adj. <kuhm-PLAY-suhnt>

_____

_____

_____

IDIOSYNCRATIC
adj. <id-ee-oh-sin-KRAT-ik>

_____

_____

_____

_____

CORDIAL
adj. <KOR-juhl>

_____

_____

_____

_____

OPULENT

rich and superior in quality

The sponsorship money changes René as he begins to enjoy a rich, **opulent** lifestyle.

Overboard
exorbitant, extravagant, lavish, luxurious, opulent

WARY

on guard, cautious, watchful

Darlene is **wary** of the sponsorship offer, she is cautious about accepting it because she worries that the money will change René.

Synonyms: vigilant

COMPLACENT

self-satisfied to the point of inactivity; unconcerned

René has become **complacent** after accepting the money, he is self-satisfied and doesn't care about racing any more.

Synonyms: smug

IDIOSYNCRATIC

peculiar to an individual

Bird of Prey's routine is **idiosyncratic**, he is surely the only speedwalker who warms up that way.

Word Alert: An *idiosyncrasy* is an idiosyncratic characteristic or behavior.

CORDIAL

friendly, warm, polite

Bird of Prey is **cordial** after the race, unlike René he is friendly and polite.

BFF
amiable, affable, amicable, camaraderie, cordial, genial

CANTANKEROUS
adj. <can-TANK-er-uhs>

_____

_____

_____

_____

CANTANKEROUS

ill-tempered

René is **cantankerous** after losing, quickly becoming ill-tempered and angry.

Fight Club
belligerent, cantankerous, contend, irate, pugnacious

AVARICE
n. <AV-uh-riss>

_____

_____

_____

_____

AVARICE

greed

Without Darlene, René's **avarice** consumes him and he greedily obsesses about his gold.

DECRY
v. <di-CRY>

_____

_____

_____

_____

DECRY

to condemn openly

René **decried** Darlene's relationship with Bird of Prey, condemning them openly as they walked down the street.

Trash Talk
belittle, decry, denigrate, denounce, deprecate, deride, disparage, vilify

---

PRECIPITOUS
adj. <pri-SIP-i-tuhs>

_____

_____

_____

_____

PRECIPITOUS

extremely steep

At the edge of the rooftop was a **precipitous** drop, straight down to the ground.

BENEVOLENT
adj. <buh-NEV-uh-luhnt>

_____

_____

_____

_____

BENEVOLENT

inclined to perform kind acts

Darlene is **benevolent**, always performing kind acts for René.

Synonyms: magnanimous

DISDAIN
n. <dis-DAYN>

_____

_____

_____

_____

DISDAIN

intense dislike

Looking at the photo with **disdain**, René utterly hates everything about Bird of Prey.

Bad Blood
abhor, acrimony, animosity, antagonistic, contempt, disdain, enmity, rancor, scorn

Word Alert: Disdain can also be a verb meaning *to dislike intensely.*

INSOLENT
adj. <IN-suh-luhnt>

_____

_____

_____

_____

INSOLENT

disrespectfully arrogant

Before the race, René is **insolent**, arrogantly mocking Bird of Prey.

Synonyms: audacity

GRATUITOUS
adj. <gruh-TOO-i-tuhs>

_____

_____

_____

_____

GRATUITOUS

unnecessary

René's **gratuitous** celebration seems excessive and unneccessary.

Synonyms: superfluous

STEADFAST
adj. <STED-fast>

_____

_____

_____

_____

STEADFAST

firm and dependable

Despite René's pleas to come back to him, Darlene remains **steadfast** and is determined to stay with Bird of Prey.

Synonyms: resolute

SOMBER
adj. <SOM-ber>

_____

_____

_____

_____

_____

SOMBER

gloomy

Even after winning, René is **somber**, gloomy and sad because Darlene will not come back to him.

Serious Business
earnest, solemn, somber

JOHNNY HIGHTOWER PART 1

Taken captive by a menacing crime lord, Special Agent Hightower finds himself in grave danger.

SOLICITOUS	anxious or concerned
HAMPER	to prevent the movement or action of
ASTUTE	having sharp judgment
INSIPID	lacking flavor or zest; dull
VINDICTIVE	seeking revenge
TERSE	expressing much in few words
GRANDIOSE	falsely exaggerating one's worth
EQUIVOCAL	uncertain, vague, misleading
IRATE	enraged
EUPHEMISM	the substitution of inoffensive term for one considered offensive
INTRANSIGENT	uncompromising
AMBIVALENT	having opposing feelings; uncertain
ARBITRARY	determined by impulse or chance, without reason
STOIC	seemingly unaffected by pleasure or pain
DENIGRATE	to attack the reputation of
ERADICATE	to eliminate
ACUITY	sharp perception or vision
NEGLIGENT	guilty of neglect
PRUDENT	wise; careful
ELUSIVE	tending to escape

SOLICITOUS
adj. <suh-LIH-si-tuhs>

_____

_____

_____

_____

SOLICITOUS

anxious or concerned

Agent Nichols anxiously paced back and forth, acting like a **solicitous** parent in her concern for Johnny Hightower's safety.

HAMPER
v. <HAM-per>

_____

_____

_____

_____

HAMPER

to prevent the movement or action of

The ropes **hampered** Johnny's efforts to escape; tying him to the chair prevented him from moving his arms and legs.

Road Block
hamper, hinder, impede, inhibit, thwart

ASTUTE
adj. <uh-STOOT>

_____

_____

_____

_____

ASTUTE

having sharp judgment

Always **astute**, Johnny Hightower used the clues around him and his sharp judgment to conclude that he was being held by a crime family in Southern Belarus.

Eagle Eye
acuity, astute, discern, incisive, keen, perspicacity

INSIPID
adj. <in-SIP-id>

_____

_____

_____

_____

INSIPID

lacking flavor or zest; dull

The **insipid** meal prompted Johnny to complain that it had no taste and needed some spicing up.

Played Out
banal, hackneyed, insipid, mundane, prosaic, trite

VINDICTIVE
adj. <vin-DIK-tiv>

_____

_____

_____

_____

VINDICTIVE

seeking revenge

Seeking revenge, Fyodor confessed his **vindictive** motives for holding Johnny Hightower hostage.

TERSE
adj. <TURS>

_____

_____

_____

_____

TERSE

expressing much in few words

Johnny offered **terse** responses to Fyodor's questions: no answer was more than a few words.

Tight-Lipped
concise, laconic, reticent, succinct, terse

GRANDIOSE
adj. <gran-dee-OHS>

_____

_____

_____

_____

GRANDIOSE

falsely exaggerating one's worth

Fyodor made **grandiose** claims about his power and, continuing to exaggerate, insisted that his family is involved in every aspect of organized crime around the world.

Cocky
bombastic, condescend, grandiose, haughty, patronize, pompous, pretentious

---

EQUIVOCAL
adj. <eh-QUI-vo-cal>

_____

_____

_____

_____

EQUIVOCAL

uncertain, vague, misleading

Despite the threats and repeated questions, Johnny offered nothing but vague and **equivocal** answers.

What the—?
abstruse, ambiguous, amorphous, enigmatic, equivocal, esoteric, nebulous

Word Alert: To *equivocate* is to speak equivocally.
Word Alert: If the prefix *un-* means *not*, what would *unequivocal* mean?

IRATE
adj. <eye-RAYT>

_____

_____

_____

_____

IRATE

enraged

Enraged that he could not make Johnny talk, Fyodor quickly became **irate**.

Fight Club
belligerent, cantankerous, contend, irate, pugnacious

EUPHEMISM
n. <YOO-fuh-mi-zm>

_____

_____

_____

_____

EUPHEMISM

the substitution of inoffensive term for one considered offensive

Fyodor used the phrase "enhanced interrogation techniques" instead of "torture" to make it seem less painful, but the **euphemism** could not hide the terrible truth of what was about to happen.

INTRANSIGENT
adj. <in-TRAN-si-juhnt>

_____

_____

_____

INTRANSIGENT

uncompromising

Johnny stood firm and would not compromise, remaining **intransigent** despite the threat of torture.

Pig-Headed
dogged, dogmatic, intransigent, obdurate, obstinate, tenacity

---

AMBIVALENT
adj. <am-BIV-uh-lent>

_____

_____

_____

AMBIVALENT

having opposing feelings; uncertain

With so many ways to torture Johnny, Fyodor was uncertain which to choose; he was **ambivalent** about whether to use the hammer, the knife or the salami.

ARBITRARY
adj. <AHR-bi-trer-ee>

_____

_____

_____

ARBITRARY

determined by impulse or chance, without reason

Fyodor used eenie meenie miney mo to decide how best to torture Johnny, randomly selecting his weapon in an **arbitrary** fashion.

Unpredictable
arbitrary, capricious, erratic, impetuous, mercurial, mutable, volatile, whimsical

---

STOIC
adj. <STOW-ik>

_____

_____

_____

STOIC

seemingly unaffected by pleasure or pain

Johnny's face remained **stoic** and he did not seem to be affected by the painful music blasting in his ears.

Synonyms: impassive

DENIGRATE
v. <DEH-ni-grate>

_____

_____

_____

_____

DENIGRATE

to attack the reputation of

Johnny **denigrated** Fyodor for his pathetic attempts at torture, attacking Fyodor's reputation as a brutal criminal.

Trash Talk
belittle, decry, denigrate, denounce, deprecate, deride, disparage, vilify

ERADICATE
v. <ih-RAD-ih-kayt>

_____
_____
_____
_____

ERADICATE

to eliminate

Fyodor plans to eliminate Johnny just like he **eradicated** the fly on the wall.

ACUITY
n. <uh-KYOO-i-tee>

_____
_____
_____
_____

ACUITY

sharp perception or vision

With startling acuity, Johnny was able to use his sharp perception to identify a specific chemical from across the room.

Eagle Eye
acuity, astute, discern, incisive, keen, perspicacity

Word Alert: to be *acute* is to demonstrate acuity

NEGLIGENT
adj. <NEG-li-juhnt>

_____
_____
_____
_____

NEGLIGENT

guilty of neglect

Fyodor was **negligent** when he left Johnny alone; he failed to make sure Johnny could not escape.

Word Alert: Don't confuse this word with *negligible*.

PRUDENT
adj. <PROO-dent>

_____
_____
_____
_____

PRUDENT

wise; careful

Johnny wants to shoot his way out of the compound but Agent Daas wisely recommends the more **prudent** option of taking the safe route out through the tunnels.

Wise Guy
circumspect, discreet, judicious, prudent, sagacious, shrewd

Word Alert: If the prefix *im-* means *not*, what would *imprudent* mean?

ELUSIVE
adj. <ih-LOO-siv>

_____
_____
_____
_____

ELUSIVE

tending to escape

Johnny is **elusive**; despite Fyodor's efforts to catch him, Johnny is able to evade capture and escape.

Gone with the Wind
elusive, ephemeral, evanescent, evasive, transient, transitory

Word Alert: To *elude* is to be elusive.

JOHNNY HIGHTOWER PART 2

Agent Nichols is sent to rescue Johnny as he tries to return safely to America.

PROPAGATE	to transmit or cause to broaden or spread
EXORBITANT	excessive
ATROPHY	to waste away
CONTEND	to compete; to argue
CIRCUMSPECT	cautious and wise
EXACERBATE	to make more severe
ALLEVIATE	to make more bearable
ALTRUISTIC	unselfishly concerned for the welfare of others
DISPARITY	the state of being different
VINDICATE	to clear of blame or suspicion
DEARTH	a scarce supply
UTILITARIAN	having only a useful function; practical
PRETENTIOUS	claiming unjust standing
PROFOUND	deep; far-reaching
COMPROMISE	to expose to danger or suspicion
COHERENT	logically connected; making sense
PROVOCATIVE	tending to stir to anger or action
ANACHRONISTIC	in the wrong time period
INDICT	to accuse of wrongdoing
IMPECCABLE	perfect

PROPAGATE
v. <PROP-uh-gayt>

_____

_____

_____

_____

PROPAGATE

to transmit or cause to broaden or spread

Seeking to **propagate** the offer of a huge reward for Johnny's capture, his enemies put up posters and spread the word from Warsaw to Riga.

Word Alert: Propaganda is information that is propagated for the purpose of promoting some cause.

EXORBITANT
adj. <eg-ZAWR-bi-tuhnt>

_____

_____

_____

_____

EXORBITANT

excessive

The bounty offered for Johnny's capture was **exorbitant**; a $750 million reward was certainly excessive.

Overboard
exorbitant, extravagant, lavish, luxurious, opulent

ATROPHY
v. <A-truh-fee>

_____

_____

_____

_____

ATROPHY

to waste away

Because Johnny had not used his legs for such a long time while in prison, the muscles **atrophied**, wasting away to almost nothing.

Word Alert: Atrophy can also be a noun meaning *a state of wasting away.*

CONTEND
v. <kuhn-TEND>

_____

_____

_____

_____

CONTEND

to compete; to argue

Contending he should be the one to save Johnny Hightower, Agent Daas challenged Nichols to compete in a game of roshambo to decide who should go to Belarus.

Fight Club
belligerent, cantankerous, contend, irate, pugnacious

Word Alert: A *contentious* person is one who contends a lot.

CIRCUMSPECT
adj. <SUR-kuhm-spekt>

_____

_____

_____

_____

CIRCUMSPECT

cautious and wise

Nichols is **circumspect** when tending to Johnny, cautiously checking all his vitals before allowing him to move.

Wise Guy
circumspect, discreet, judicious, prudent, sagacious, shrewd

EXACERBATE

v. <ex-ASS-er-bate>

_____

_____

_____

_____

EXACERBATE

to make more severe

Though trying to help, Nichols **exacerbated** Johnny's pain, making it worse when she poured acid on the wound.

ALLEVIATE

v. <uh-LEE-vee-ate>

_____

_____

_____

_____

ALLEVIATE

to make more bearable

The plant's medicinal powers helped to **alleviate** Johnny's pain and make it more bearable.

Feel Better
alleviate, mitigate, mollify, temper

ALTRUISTIC

adj. <al-troo-IS-tik>

_____

_____

_____

_____

ALTRUISTIC

unselfishly concerned for the welfare of others

Nichols informed Johnny of her **altruistic** motives for becoming an agent; having witnessed a lot of crime growing up, she decided to leave everything else behind and devote her life to helping people.

Word Alert: Altruism is altruistic behavior.

DISPARITY

n. <di-SPAIR-i-tee>

_____

_____

_____

_____

DISPARITY

the state of being different

Johnny uncovered a **disparity** between Nichols' official record and her own account of where she said she was born, a difference that makes him suspicious.

Synonyms: discrepancy

Word Alert: Something *disparate* possesses a disparity.

VINDICATE

v. <VIN-di-kayt>

_____

_____

_____

_____

VINDICATE

to clear of blame or suspicion

Nichols is **vindicated** when she shows Johnny her passport; she is cleared of suspicion because while born in Paris, she grew up in Philadelphia.

Synonyms: exonerate

DEARTH
n. <DURTH>

_____

_____

_____

_____

DEARTH

a scarce supply

There was a **dearth** of berries because of the dry winter; with hardly a single berry in sight.

UTILITARIAN
adj. <yoo-til-i-TAIR-ee-uhn>

_____

_____

_____

_____

UTILITARIAN

having only a useful function; practical

Johnny's watch is certainly **utilitarian**: its useful functions include boiling water, checking sports scores, and even finding dinner.

Synonyms: pragmatic

PRETENTIOUS
adj. <prih-TEN-shuhs>

_____

_____

_____

_____

PRETENTIOUS

claiming unjust standing

Agent Nichols is **pretentious**; despite being a trained field agent she refuses to drink water from the stream and claims she must have sparkling bottled water.

Cocky
bombastic, condescend, grandiose, haughty, patronize, pompous, pretentious

Word Alert: A *pretense* is false appearance.

PROFOUND
adj. <pruh-FOUND>

_____

_____

_____

_____

PROFOUND

deep; far-reaching

Impressed by his deep thoughts on life and death, Nichols tells Johnny he should turn his **profound** words into a book..

Word Alert: Profundity is the state of being profound.

COMPROMISE
v. <KOM-pruh-mize>

_____

_____

_____

_____

COMPROMISE

to expose to danger or suspicion

Johnny's safety is **compromised** when Nichols' loud radio goes off; in range of his potential captors, he is exposed to great danger.

COHERENT
adj. <co-HEER-ent>

_____

_____

_____

_____

COHERENT

logically connected; making sense

Forming a **coherent**, logical argument, Johnny explained the case against Nichols so forcefully it was impossible to dispute.

Word Alert: To *cohere* is to make something coherent or to stick together.
Word Alert: If the prefix *in-* means *not*, what would *incoherent* mean?

PROVOCATIVE
adj. <pruh-VAWK-uh-tiv>

_____

_____

_____

_____

PROVOCATIVE

tending to stir to anger or action

Nichols' **provocative** remarks about America angered Johnny; after hearing them, he was ready to take her down.

Synonyms: inflammatory

Word Alert: To *provoke* is to be provocative.

ANACHRONISTIC
adj. <uh-nak-ruh-NIS-tik>

_____

_____

_____

_____

ANACHRONISTIC

in the wrong time period

Johnny's bow-and-arrow is **anachronistic**; it is an out-dated weapon last used in combat centuries ago.

Word Alert: An *anachronism* is something that is anachronistic.

INDICT
v. <in-DITE>

_____

_____

_____

_____

INDICT

to accuse of wrongdoing

Nichols was **indicted** on multiple charges, including treason, larceny, and possession of a firearm in a school disctrict.

IMPECCABLE
adj. <im-PEK-uh-buhl>

_____

_____

_____

_____

IMPECCABLE

perfect

Nichols is amazed by Johnny's **impeccable** appearance; he emerges from behind the bush looking perfect in a suit and tie.

STRANDED! PART 4

Thirty years later Brett and Katie are still stranded on the island but now they finally get some answers.

PLIABLE	easily bent or shaped
COGNIZANT	aware
MITIGATE	to lessen in force or intensity
PROLIFERATE	to increase or spread at a rapid rate
HERETICAL	characterized by departure from accepted beliefs or standards
GREGARIOUS	sociable
CONSCIENTIOUS	thorough and careful
FRUGAL	careful with money, stingy
ESTEEM	to value highly, to respect
AMORPHOUS	lacking definite form
PROVINCIAL	narrow-minded
EVANESCENT	fading away
AFFLUENT	wealthy
CAPRICIOUS	impulsive, unpredictable
INHERENT	naturally occurring; essential
CREDIBLE	believable
AUGMENT	to make greater in size or quantity
PREVALENT	widely occurring
LUXURIOUS	rich and superior in quality
INDULGE	to please or satisfy

PLIABLE
adj. <PLY-uh-buhl>

_____

_____

_____

_____

PLIABLE

easily bent or shaped

The metal rod was surprisingly **pliable**, bending easily in Katie's hands.

Word Alert: *Pliant* also means easily bendable or flexible.

COGNIZANT
adj. <KOG-nuh-zuhnt>

_____

_____

_____

_____

COGNIZANT

aware

Touching the magic rod made Brett **cognizant** of its origin, and he is now aware of what exactly it is and how it got there.

MITIGATE
v. <MIT-ih-gayt>

_____

_____

_____

_____

MITIGATE

to lessen in force or intensity

The ice helped **mitigate** Natalio's pain, relieving him of his discomfort.

Feel Better
alleviate, mitigate, mollify, temper

PROLIFERATE
v. <pruh-LIF-uh-rayt>

_____

_____

_____

_____

PROLIFERATE

to increase or spread at a rapid rate

The video of Max defeating Natalio **proliferated** across the Internet; it spread very rapidly.

HERETICAL
adj. <huh-REHT-i-kul>

_____

_____

_____

_____

HERETICAL

characterized by departure from accepted beliefs or standards

Bruno believes that it would be **heretical** for an Italian to train a Frenchman since the countries have an established hatred.

Word Alert: A *heretic* is someone who holds heretical opinions.

GREGARIOUS
adj. <gri-GAIR-ee-uhs>

_____

_____

_____

_____

GREGARIOUS

sociable

Bird of Prey is extremely **gregarious** and sociable; he loves parties and interacting with people.

Synonyms: convivial

CONSCIENTIOUS
adj. <con-shee-EN-shuhs>

_____

_____

_____

_____

CONSCIENTIOUS

thorough and careful

Bruno was very **conscientious** in putting together Natalio's trip itinerary; he thoughtfully planned for everything Natalio might need along the way.

Synonyms: meticulous, scrupulous

FRUGAL
adj. <FROO-guhl>

_____

_____

_____

_____

FRUGAL

careful with money, stingy

Refusing to spend any money, René lives a **frugal** existence.

ESTEEM
v. <ih-STEEM>

_____

_____

_____

_____

ESTEEM

to value highly, to respect

Natalio and René **esteem** one another, respecting each other for their talents and mutual good looks.

Synonyms: revere

Word Alert: Esteem can also be a noun meaning *respect.*

AMORPHOUS
adj. <uh-MOR-fuhs>

_____

_____

_____

_____

AMORPHOUS

lacking definite form

René prefers to work with the **amorphous** putty, which can easily be changed because it lacks any definitive form.

What the—?
abstruse, ambiguous, amorphous, enigmatic, equivocal, esoteric, nebulous

PROVINCIAL
adj. <pruh-VIN-shuhl>

_____
_____
_____

PROVINCIAL

narrow-minded

René's narrow-minded, **provincial** mentality leads him to trust his superstitious beliefs in omens and curses over logic and reasoning.

Synonyms: insular

EVANESCENT
adj. <ev-uh-NES-uhnt>

_____
_____
_____

EVANESCENT

fading away

An **evanescent** Max Wind mysteriously appears to tell Brett and Katie how he got to the island, before quickly vanishing into thin air.

Gone with the Wind
elusive, ephemeral, evanescent, evasive, transient, transitory

---

AFFLUENT
adj. <AF-loo-uhnt>

_____
_____
_____
_____

AFFLUENT

wealthy

The **affluent** Natalio Belastracci boasts of his riches, telling Max Wind of the many islands, yachts, and hotels that he owns.

CAPRICIOUS
adj. <kuh-PREE-shuhs>

_____
_____
_____

CAPRICIOUS

impulsive, unpredictable

Natalio makes **capricious**, impulsive decisions about the details of the race.

Unpredictable
arbitrary, capricious, erratic, impetuous, mercurial, mutable, volatile, whimsical

Word Alert: A *caprice* is a capricious change of mind.

INHERENT
adj. <in-HEER-uhnt>

_____
_____
_____
_____

INHERENT

naturally occurring; essential

Having speedwalked out of his mother's womb, René was clearly born with an **inherent** speedwalking talent.

Synonyms: innate

CREDIBLE

adj. <KRED-uh-buhl>

_____

_____

_____

_____

CREDIBLE

believable

The video tape offered believable, **credible** proof, confirming that Max had, indeed, defeated René.

Word Alert: If the prefix *in-* means *not*, what would *incredible* mean?

AUGMENT

v. <awg-MENT>

_____

_____

_____

_____

AUGMENT

to make greater in size or quantity

Bruno **augmented** the dessert, adding several more scoops of ice cream and a cherry.

PREVALENT

adj. <PREH-va-lent>

_____

_____

_____

_____

PREVALENT

widely occurring

Loneliness is **prevalent** among speedwalkers; it is quite common for them to end up alone.

LUXURIOUS

adj. <luhg-ZHOOR-ee-uhs>

_____

_____

_____

_____

LUXURIOUS

rich and superior in quality

Brett and Katie discover Natalio's lavish, **luxurious** hotel that includes swimming pools, a spa, and even a bowling alley.

Overboard
exorbitant, extravagant, lavish, luxurious, opulent

INDULGE

v. <in-DUHLJ>

_____

_____

_____

_____

INDULGE

to please or satisfy

Brett and Katie **indulge** themselves by devouring the ice cream, delighting in every bite.

Word Alert: *Indulgent* means tending to indulge.

APPENDIX A: ALPHABETIC WORD LIST

ABHOR	*The Artists Part 1*	BOLSTER	*Imaginary Larry*
ABSTINENCE	*The Artists Part 1*	BOMBASTIC	*Mad Scientists Part 2*
ABSTRUSE	*Shall We Dance? Part 2*	BRAZEN	*Speedwalkers: The Rise and Fall of René Dupont*
ACCLAIM	*Stranded! Part 2*	BRUSQUE	*Mad Scientists Part 2*
ACCORD	*The Artists Part 2*	BUOYANT	*Stranded! Part 3*
ACERBIC	*The Artists Part 1*	BURGEON	*Imaginary Larry: The Battle for Desert Malaguay*
ACRIMONY	*Two's Company 3*	BUTTRESS	*The Study Partner*
ACUITY	*Johnny Hightower Part 1*	CACOPHONY	*Rumor Chick: The Diary*
ADEPT	*Shall We Dance? Part 3*	CAJOLE	*Stranded! Part 2*
ADMONISH	*Rumor Chick: The New Guy*	CALLOUS	*Imaginary Larry: The Fellowship of the Meyerson*
ADORN	*Imaginary Larry*	CAMARADERIE	*Imaginary Larry*
ADROIT	*Stranded! Part 2*	CANDID	*The Artists Part 1*
ADULATION	*Rumor Chick: The New Guy*	CANTANKEROUS	*Speedwalkers: The Legend of Max Wind*
ADVERSITY	*Shall We Dance? Part 2*	CAPRICIOUS	*Stranded! Part 4*
ADVOCATE	*Imaginary Larry*	CARNIVOROUS	*Imaginary Larry*
AESTHETIC	*The Artists Part 1*	CATHARTIC	*Speedwalkers: The Rise and Fall of René Dupont*
AFFABLE	*Shall We Dance? Part 1*	CAUSTIC	*Shall We Dance? Part 3*
AFFLUENT	*Stranded! Part 4*	CENSURE	*Two's Company 1*
ALACRITY	*Mad Scientists Part 2*	CEREBRAL	*Shall We Dance? Part 2*
ALIENATE	*Imaginary Larry: The Battle for Desert Malaguay*	CHRONIC	*Speedwalkers: The Rise and Fall of René Dupont*
ALLEVIATE	*Johnny Hightower Part 2*	CIRCUITOUS	*Imaginary Larry: The Fellowship of the Meyerson*
ALTRUISTIC	*Johnny Hightower Part 2*	CIRCUMSPECT	*Johnny Hightower Part 2*
AMALGAM	*The Artists Part 1*	CIRCUMVENT	*Rumor Chick: The Diary*
AMBIGUOUS	*Imaginary Larry*	CLAIRVOYANCE	*Rumor Chick: The Diary*
AMBIVALENT	*Johnny Hightower Part 1*	CLANDESTINE	*Shall We Dance? Part 2*
AMELIORATE	*Imaginary Larry: The Fellowship of the Meyerson*	COGENT	*Shall We Dance? Part 3*
AMENABLE	*Imaginary Larry: The Battle for Desert Malaguay*	COGNIZANT	*Stranded! Part 4*
AMIABLE	*The Study Partner*	COHERENT	*Johnny Hightower Part 2*
AMICABLE	*Imaginary Larry: The Fellowship of the Meyerson*	COHESIVE	*Imaginary Larry: The Battle for Desert Malaguay*
AMORPHOUS	*Stranded! Part 4*	COLLABORATE	*The Artists Part 1*
ANACHRONISTIC	*Johnny Hightower Part 2*	COMMEND	*Two's Company 3*
ANECDOTE	*Mad Scientists Part 1*	COMPEL	*Stranded! Part 2*
ANIMOSITY	*Stranded! Part 1*	COMPETENT	*Shall We Dance? Part 1*
ANTAGONISTIC	*The Artists Part 2*	COMPLACENT	*Speedwalkers: The Legend of Max Wind*
APATHETIC	*Speedwalkers: The Legend of Max Wind*	COMPLICITY	*Rumor Chick: The New Guy*
APPEASE	*Imaginary Larry*	COMPOSED	*Two's Company 3*
APPREHENSIVE	*Stranded! Part 3*	COMPROMISE	*Johnny Hightower Part 2*
ARBITRARY	*Johnny Hightower Part 1*	CONCEDE	*Rumor Chick: The New Guy*
ARCHAIC	*Rumor Chick: The Diary*	CONCILIATE	*Stranded! Part 2*
ARDOR	*Stranded! Part 2*	CONCISE	*The Artists Part 2*
ARID	*Imaginary Larry: The Fellowship of the Meyerson*	CONCORD	*Two's Company 1*
ARTICULATE	*Shall We Dance? Part 3*	CONCUR	*Rumor Chick: The New Guy*
ASCERTAIN	*Rumor Chick: The New Guy*	CONDESCEND	*Two's Company 3*
ASPIRE	*Two's Company 1*	CONDONE	*Shall We Dance? Part 2*
ASSESS	*Two's Company 1*	CONFORM	*Shall We Dance? Part 2*
ASSIDUOUS	*Rumor Chick: The New Guy*	CONFOUND	*The Study Partner*
ASTUTE	*Johnny Hightower Part 1*	CONJECTURE	*Mad Scientists Part 2*
ATROPHY	*Johnny Hightower Part 2*	CONSCIENTIOUS	*Stranded! Part 4*
AUDACITY	*Mad Scientists Part 1*	CONSENSUS	*Imaginary Larry: The Battle for Desert Malaguay*
AUGMENT	*Stranded! Part 4*	CONSOLIDATE	*Stranded! Part 1*
AUSPICIOUS	*Mad Scientists Part 1*	CONSTITUENT	*Imaginary Larry: The Battle for Desert Malaguay*
AUSTERE	*Shall We Dance? Part 2*	CONSTRAIN	*Shall We Dance? Part 2*
AUTONOMY	*The Artists Part 1*	CONSTRUE	*Imaginary Larry*
AVARICE	*Speedwalkers: The Legend of Max Wind*	CONTEMPT	*Speedwalkers: The Rise and Fall of René Dupont*
AVERSE	*Two's Company 4*	CONTEND	*Johnny Hightower Part 2*
AWE	*The Artists Part 2*	CONTRITE	*Mad Scientists Part 2*
BANAL	*Shall We Dance? Part 1*	CONTRIVED	*Shall We Dance? Part 1*
BANE	*Two's Company 4*	CONVIVIAL	*Shall We Dance? Part 1*
BELIE	*The Artists Part 1*	CONVOLUTED	*Two's Company 4*
BELITTLE	*Rumor Chick: The Diary*	COPIOUS	*Stranded! Part 3*
BELLIGERENT	*Imaginary Larry: The Battle for Desert Malaguay*	CORDIAL	*Speedwalkers: The Legend of Max Wind*
BEMUSE	*Rumor Chick: The New Guy*	CORROBORATE	*Shall We Dance? Part 3*
BENEVOLENT	*Speedwalkers: The Legend of Max Wind*	CREDIBLE	*Stranded! Part 4*
BENIGN	*Rumor Chick: The Diary*	CUNNING	*Rumor Chick: The New Guy*
BERATE	*The Artists Part 2*	CURSORY	*Two's Company 4*
BOISTEROUS	*Shall We Dance? Part 3*	CURTAIL	*Two's Company 2*

CYNICAL	Shall We Dance? Part 3
DAUNT	Two's Company 3
DEARTH	Johnny Hightower Part 2
DEBILITATE	Two's Company 2
DEBUNK	Stranded! Part 3
DECORUM	Mad Scientists Part 2
DECRY	Speedwalkers: The Legend of Max Wind
DEFER	Two's Company 4
DELETERIOUS	Imaginary Larry
DELINEATE	The Artists Part 2
DEMEAN	Mad Scientists Part 2
DENIGRATE	Johnny Hightower Part 1
DENOUNCE	Imaginary Larry: The Battle for Desert Malaguay
DEPRECATE	Shall We Dance? Part 1
DERIDE	Speedwalkers: The Rise and Fall of René Dupont
DESPAIR	Two's Company 4
DESPONDENT	Stranded! Part 3
DETER	Two's Company 2
DIFFIDENCE	Mad Scientists Part 2
DIGRESS	Imaginary Larry: The Fellowship of the Meyerson
DILATORY	Two's Company 3
DILIGENT	Two's Company 1
DIMINUTIVE	Mad Scientists Part 1
DISCERN	Imaginary Larry
DISCORD	Two's Company 2
DISCREDIT	Shall We Dance? Part 3
DISCREET	Mad Scientists Part 2
DISCREPANCY	Shall We Dance? Part 2
DISCRETE	Imaginary Larry
DISDAIN	Speedwalkers: The Legend of Max Wind
DISGRUNTLED	Mad Scientists Part 1
DISMISS	Rumor Chick: The Diary
DISPARAGE	Two's Company 4
DISPARITY	Johnny Hightower Part 2
DISPASSIONATE	Shall We Dance? Part 3
DISPEL	The Study Partner
DISPOSITION	Shall We Dance? Part 1
DISSEMBLE	Shall We Dance? Part 3
DISSEMINATE	Two's Company 1
DISSENT	Imaginary Larry: The Battle for Desert Malaguay
DISSIPATE	Rumor Chick: The Diary
DIVERGENT	Two's Company 2
DIVISIVE	Imaginary Larry: The Fellowship of the Meyerson
DIVULGE	Speedwalkers: The Rise and Fall of René Dupont
DOCILE	Mad Scientists Part 2
DOGGED	Speedwalkers: The Rise and Fall of René Dupont
DOGMATIC	Two's Company 4
DOUR	Speedwalkers: The Rise and Fall of René Dupont
DUBIOUS	The Artists Part 2
DUPLICITY	Stranded! Part 2
EARNEST	The Study Partner
EBULLIENT	Mad Scientists Part 1
ECCENTRIC	The Artists Part 1
ECLECTIC	Two's Company 3
ECSTASY	Two's Company 3
EFFACE	Stranded! Part 1
EFFICACIOUS	The Artists Part 2
EFFUSIVE	Mad Scientists Part 2
ELATED	Imaginary Larry
ELITE	Two's Company 4
ELOQUENT	Two's Company 3
ELUCIDATE	Stranded! Part 3
ELUSIVE	Johnny Hightower Part 1
EMBELLISH	Shall We Dance? Part 1
EMINENT	Shall We Dance? Part 2
EMPIRICAL	Stranded! Part 1
EMULATE	The Artists Part 1
ENCOMPASS	Imaginary Larry
ENCROACH	The Study Partner
ENERVATE	Speedwalkers: The Rise and Fall of René Dupont
ENHANCE	Stranded! Part 3
ENIGMATIC	The Study Partner
ENMITY	Two's Company 4
ENTHRALL	The Artists Part 1
ENTICE	Shall We Dance? Part 1
ENTRENCH	Imaginary Larry: The Battle for Desert Malaguay
ENUMERATE	Speedwalkers: The Legend of Max Wind
ENUNCIATE	Two's Company 4
EPHEMERAL	Shall We Dance? Part 3
EQUANIMITY	Two's Company 2
EQUIVOCAL	Johnny Hightower Part 1
ERADICATE	Johnny Hightower Part 1
ERRATIC	Mad Scientists Part 2
ERUDITE	Mad Scientists Part 1
ESOTERIC	Shall We Dance? Part 1
ESPOUSE	Imaginary Larry: The Fellowship of the Meyerson
ESTEEM	Stranded! Part 4
ESTRANGE	Rumor Chick: The New Guy
EULOGY	Stranded! Part 3
EUPHEMISM	Johnny Hightower Part 1
EUPHORIA	Speedwalkers: The Rise and Fall of René Dupont
EVANESCENT	Stranded! Part 4
EVASIVE	Two's Company 4
EVOKE	Imaginary Larry: The Battle for Desert Malaguay
EXACERBATE	Johnny Hightower Part 2
EXACTING	Mad Scientists Part 1
EXALT	Two's Company 1
EXASPERATE	Stranded! Part 1
EXEMPLARY	Speedwalkers: The Legend of Max Wind
EXONERATE	Two's Company 4
EXORBITANT	Johnny Hightower Part 2
EXPEDITE	Stranded! Part 3
EXPLOIT	Stranded! Part 1
EXTOL	Stranded! Part 3
EXTRAVAGANT	Imaginary Larry: The Battle for Desert Malaguay
EXUBERANT	Stranded! Part 3
FACILE	Imaginary Larry
FACILITATE	Shall We Dance? Part 1
FATUOUS	Stranded! Part 1
FEASIBLE	Stranded! Part 3
FELICITY	Two's Company 4
FERVENT	Two's Company 3
FLAGRANT	Speedwalkers: The Rise and Fall of René Dupont
FLAMBOYANT	Two's Company 1
FLORID	Imaginary Larry
FLOURISH	Stranded! Part 1
FORTHRIGHT	Mad Scientists Part 2
FOSTER	Mad Scientists Part 1
FRENETIC	Two's Company 4
FRIVOLOUS	Speedwalkers: The Rise and Fall of René Dupont
FRUGAL	Stranded! Part 4
FUTILE	Stranded! Part 2
GALVANIZE	The Artists Part 1
GARISH	Two's Company 1
GARRULOUS	Imaginary Larry
GENIAL	Rumor Chick: The Diary
GRANDIOSE	Johnny Hightower Part 1
GRATE	Imaginary Larry
GRATUITOUS	Speedwalkers: The Legend of Max Wind
GREGARIOUS	Stranded! Part 4
GUILE	Two's Company 4
HACKNEYED	Imaginary Larry: The Battle for Desert Malaguay
HAIL	Two's Company 4
HAMPER	Johnny Hightower Part 1
HARANGUE	The Study Partner
HAUGHTY	Two's Company 1
HEED	Imaginary Larry
HERETICAL	Stranded! Part 4
HINDER	Mad Scientists Part 1
HOMOGENEOUS	Stranded! Part 3

IDIOSYNCRATIC	*Speedwalkers: The Legend of Max Wind*
ILLICIT	*Mad Scientists Part 2*
ILLUSORY	*Stranded! Part 2*
IMPARTIAL	*Two's Company 2*
IMPASSIONED	*Shall We Dance? Part 1*
IMPASSIVE	*Stranded! Part 2*
IMPECCABLE	*Johnny Hightower Part 2*
IMPEDE	*Speedwalkers: The Rise and Fall of René Dupont*
IMPERIOUS	*Mad Scientists Part 2*
IMPETUOUS	*Speedwalkers: The Legend of Max Wind*
IMPUGN	*Mad Scientists Part 1*
INACCESSIBLE	*The Study Partner*
INCISIVE	*Rumor Chick: The Diary*
INCONGRUOUS	*Stranded! Part 2*
INCONSEQUENTIAL	*Shall We Dance? Part 3*
INCONTROVERTIBLE	*Rumor Chick: The Diary*
INCORRIGIBLE	*Rumor Chick: The Diary*
INCREDULOUS	*Stranded! Part 3*
INDICT	*Johnny Hightower Part 2*
INDIFFERENT	*Shall We Dance? Part 1*
INDIGENOUS	*Imaginary Larry: The Fellowship of the Meyerson*
INDIGNATION	*Rumor Chick: The Diary*
INDUCE	*Two's Company 2*
INDULGE	*Stranded! Part 4*
INFLAMMATORY	*Two's Company 2*
INGENUOUS	*Imaginary Larry*
INHERENT	*Stranded! Part 4*
INHIBIT	*Shall We Dance? Part 3*
INNATE	*Shall We Dance? Part 2*
INNOCUOUS	*The Study Partner*
INNOVATIVE	*The Artists Part 1*
INQUISITIVE	*Two's Company 2*
INSINUATE	*Shall We Dance? Part 2*
INSIPID	*Johnny Hightower Part 1*
INSOLENT	*Speedwalkers: The Legend of Max Wind*
INSTIGATE	*Imaginary Larry: The Battle for Desert Malaguay*
INSULAR	*Imaginary Larry: The Fellowship of the Meyerson*
INTELLIGIBLE	*Mad Scientists Part 2*
INTRANSIGENT	*Johnny Hightower Part 1*
INUNDATE	*Two's Company 1*
INVIGORATE	*Speedwalkers: The Rise and Fall of René Dupont*
INVOKE	*Imaginary Larry*
IRATE	*Johnny Hightower Part 1*
JADED	*Speedwalkers: The Rise and Fall of René Dupont*
JUDICIOUS	*The Study Partner*
JUXTAPOSE	*Two's Company 4*
KEEN	*The Study Partner*
LACONIC	*Stranded! Part 3*
LAMENT	*Stranded! Part 3*
LANGUID	*Stranded! Part 2*
LATENT	*Shall We Dance? Part 3*
LAUD	*The Artists Part 2*
LAVISH	*Imaginary Larry: The Fellowship of the Meyerson*
LUCID	*Imaginary Larry: The Fellowship of the Meyerson*
LUXURIOUS	*Stranded! Part 4*
MAGNANIMOUS	*Imaginary Larry: The Fellowship of the Meyerson*
MANDATE	*Two's Company 3*
MANIFEST	*Rumor Chick: The New Guy*
MEAGER	*The Artists Part 2*
MEDIOCRE	*Two's Company 3*
MELANCHOLY	*Two's Company 1*
MERCENARY	*Two's Company 2*
MERCURIAL	*Mad Scientists Part 1*
METICULOUS	*Two's Company 1*
MIRTH	*Shall We Dance? Part 3*
MITIGATE	*Stranded! Part 4*
MOLLIFY	*Speedwalkers: The Rise and Fall of René Dupont*
MOROSE	*Rumor Chick: The New Guy*
MUNDANE	*The Study Partner*
MUTABLE	*The Artists Part 1*

NEBULOUS	*Stranded! Part 3*
NEGLIGENT	*Johnny Hightower Part 1*
NEGLIGIBLE	*Imaginary Larry*
NONCHALANT	*Two's Company 3*
NOSTALGIA	*The Artists Part 1*
NOTORIOUS	*Rumor Chick: The New Guy*
NOVEL	*Mad Scientists Part 1*
NURTURE	*Two's Company 3*
OBDURATE	*Mad Scientists Part 1*
OBLIVIOUS	*Stranded! Part 1*
OBSOLETE	*Stranded! Part 1*
OBSTINATE	*Rumor Chick: The Diary*
OBSTREPEROUS	*Rumor Chick: The Diary*
OBTRUSIVE	*Imaginary Larry*
OBTUSE	*Shall We Dance? Part 1*
OFFICIOUS	*Shall We Dance? Part 2*
OMINOUS	*Rumor Chick: The New Guy*
OPAQUE	*The Artists Part 1*
OPPORTUNE	*Stranded! Part 2*
OPULENT	*Speedwalkers: The Legend of Max Wind*
ORNATE	*Imaginary Larry: The Battle for Desert Malaguay*
ORTHODOX	*Imaginary Larry*
PARADOX	*Two's Company 1*
PARTISAN	*Shall We Dance? Part 1*
PATRONIZE	*Rumor Chick: The Diary*
PENITENT	*Rumor Chick: The Diary*
PERNICIOUS	*The Study Partner*
PERPETUAL	*Shall We Dance? Part 2*
PERSEVERE	*Stranded! Part 2*
PERSPICACITY	*Speedwalkers: The Rise and Fall of René DuPont*
PERTINENT	*Shall We Dance? Part 2*
PERVASIVE	*Mad Scientists Part 2*
PLACID	*The Study Partner*
PLAUSIBLE	*Two's Company 4*
PLIABLE	*Stranded! Part 4*
POIGNANT	*Rumor Chick: The New Guy*
POLARIZE	*Shall We Dance? Part 3*
POMPOUS	*Speedwalkers: The Rise and Fall of René Dupont*
PRAGMATIC	*Imaginary Larry: The Battle for Desert Malaguay*
PRECARIOUS	*Rumor Chick: The Diary*
PRECIPITOUS	*Speedwalkers: The Legend of Max Wind*
PREDILECTION	*Shall We Dance? Part 3*
PRETENTIOUS	*Johnny Hightower Part 2*
PREVALENT	*Stranded! Part 4*
PRISTINE	*Stranded! Part 2*
PRODIGIOUS	*Two's Company 3*
PROFOUND	*Johnny Hightower Part 2*
PROLIFERATE	*Stranded! Part 4*
PROLIFIC	*Mad Scientists Part 1*
PROPAGATE	*Johnny Hightower Part 2*
PROPENSITY	*The Study Partner*
PROPRIETY	*Shall We Dance? Part 2*
PROSAIC	*Mad Scientists Part 1*
PROSPERITY	*Imaginary Larry: The Battle for Desert Malaguay*
PROVINCIAL	*Stranded! Part 4*
PROVOCATIVE	*Johnny Hightower Part 2*
PRUDENT	*Johnny Hightower Part 1*
PUGNACIOUS	*Mad Scientists Part 2*
QUELL	*Rumor Chick: The New Guy*
RANCOR	*Two's Company 2*
RAVENOUS	*Stranded! Part 2*
REBUKE	*Rumor Chick: The New Guy*
RECIPROCATE	*Rumor Chick: The New Guy*
RECLUSIVE	*The Artists Part 1*
RECONCILE	*Stranded! Part 1*
REFUGE	*Stranded! Part 1*
REFUTE	*Imaginary Larry*
REITERATE	*Two's Company 2*
RELINQUISH	*Imaginary Larry: The Battle for Desert Malaguay*
REMINISCE	*Two's Company 2*

RENOUNCE	*Rumor Chick: The New Guy*
REPREHENSIBLE	*Two's Company 1*
REPROACH	*Two's Company 2*
REPUDIATE	*Imaginary Larry*
RESENT	*Stranded! Part 1*
RESIGNATION	*Two's Company 3*
RESILIENT	*Speedwalkers: The Legend of Max Wind*
RESOLUTE	*Mad Scientists Part 1*
RESOLVE	*Stranded! Part 2*
RETICENT	*Shall We Dance? Part 1*
REVERE	*Mad Scientists Part 1*
REVOKE	*Stranded! Part 1*
RUDIMENTARY	*Stranded! Part 1*
SAGACIOUS	*Two's Company 1*
SANCTION	*Two's Company 2*
SANGUINE	*Two's Company 2*
SCATHING	*Two's Company 3*
SCOFF	*Stranded! Part 1*
SCORN	*Imaginary Larry*
SCRUPULOUS	*Imaginary Larry*
SCRUTINIZE	*Imaginary Larry: The Fellowship of the Meyerson*
SERENE	*Stranded! Part 1*
SHREWD	*Mad Scientists Part 1*
SKEPTICAL	*The Study Partner*
SMUG	*Mad Scientists Part 1*
SOLEMN	*Stranded! Part 3*
SOLICITOUS	*Johnny Hightower Part 1*
SOMBER	*Speedwalkers: The Legend of Max Wind*
SPECIOUS	*Imaginary Larry*
SPORADIC	*The Study Partner*
SPURIOUS	*Imaginary Larry: The Fellowship of the Meyerson*
SPURN	*Mad Scientists Part 2*
SQUANDER	*Shall We Dance? Part 2*
STAGNANT	*Shall We Dance? Part 1*
STEADFAST	*Speedwalkers: The Legend of Max Wind*
STOIC	*Johnny Hightower Part 1*
SUBDUE	*The Study Partner*
SUBSTANTIATE	*Stranded! Part 2*
SUBVERT	*Imaginary Larry: The Battle for Desert Malaguay*
SUCCINCT	*Speedwalkers: The Rise and Fall of René Dupont*
SUPERFLUOUS	*Two's Company 3*
SUPPLANT	*Rumor Chick: The New Guy*
SUPPRESS	*Stranded! Part 3*
SURREPTITIOUS	*Two's Company 1*
TACT	*Shall We Dance? Part 3*
TEDIOUS	*Two's Company 3*
TEMPER	*Imaginary Larry*
TENACITY	*Shall We Dance? Part 3*
TERSE	*Johnny Hightower Part 1*
THERAPEUTIC	*The Study Partner*
THWART	*Imaginary Larry*
TORPOR	*Shall We Dance? Part 3*
TRACTABLE	*Two's Company 2*
TRANQUIL	*The Artists Part 1*
TRANSIENT	*Two's Company 1*
TRANSITORY	*Mad Scientists Part 2*
TREACHERY	*Imaginary Larry: The Fellowship of the Meyerson*
TRITE	*Stranded! Part 2*
TRIVIAL	*Shall We Dance? Part 1*
TUMULTUOUS	*Shall We Dance? Part 1*
UNASSUMING	*Imaginary Larry: The Fellowship of the Meyerson*
UNDERMINE	*Stranded! Part 1*
UNDERSCORE	*Two's Company 1*
UNIFORM	*Shall We Dance? Part 2*
URBANE	*Two's Company 1*
USURP	*Stranded! Part 1*
UTILITARIAN	*Johnny Hightower Part 2*
VACILLATE	*Rumor Chick: The Diary*
VAPID	*Imaginary Larry: The Fellowship of the Meyerson*
VEILED	*Two's Company 2*
VENERATE	*The Artists Part 1*
VERBOSE	*Stranded! Part 2*
VERSATILE	*Two's Company 3*
VICARIOUS	*Speedwalkers: The Rise and Fall of René Dupont*
VIGILANT	*Imaginary Larry: The Fellowship of the Meyerson*
VILIFY	*Imaginary Larry: The Battle for Desert Malaguay*
VINDICATE	*Johnny Hightower Part 2*
VINDICTIVE	*Johnny Hightower Part 1*
VIVACIOUS	*Shall We Dance? Part 1*
VOLATILE	*Stranded! Part 1*
VOLUBLE	*Two's Company 2*
VOLUMINOUS	*Rumor Chick: The Diary*
VULNERABLE	*Stranded! Part 3*
WARRANT	*Two's Company 4*
WARY	*Speedwalkers: The Legend of Max Wind*
WAVER	*Shall We Dance? Part 2*
WHIMSICAL	*Shall We Dance? Part 2*
ZEALOUS	*Imaginary Larry: The Fellowship of the Meyerson*

APPENDIX B: EPISODE WORD LIST

Two's Company Part 1
- INUNDATE
- GARISH
- UNDERSCORE
- HAUGHTY
- TRANSIENT
- URBANE
- METICULOUS
- DISSEMINATE
- CENSURE
- SURREPTITIOUS
- MELANCHOLY
- ASPIRE
- CONCORD
- DILIGENT
- REPREHENSIBLE
- EXALT
- FLAMBOYANT
- ASSESS
- SAGACIOUS
- PARADOX

Two's Company Part 2
- RANCOR
- IMPARTIAL
- SANCTION
- MERCENARY
- INDUCE
- TRACTABLE
- VOLUBLE
- REITERATE
- CURTAIL
- DEBILITATE
- INFLAMMATORY
- EQUANIMITY
- DETER
- VEILED
- DISCORD
- INQUISITIVE
- DIVERGENT
- REPROACH
- REMINISCE
- SANGUINE

Two's Company Part 3
- NONCHALANT
- DILATORY
- SUPERFLUOUS
- CONDESCEND
- ACRIMONY
- PRODIGIOUS
- DAUNT
- TEDIOUS
- MEDIOCRE
- MANDATE
- RESIGNATION
- NURTURE
- FERVENT
- ECLECTIC
- COMPOSED
- VERSATILE
- SCATHING
- ELOQUENT
- COMMEND
- ECSTASY

Two's Company Part 4
- DESPAIR
- EXONERATE
- JUXTAPOSE
- EVASIVE
- CURSORY
- DISPARAGE
- ELITE
- BANE
- DEFER
- AVERSE
- ENMITY
- GUILE
- DOGMATIC
- WARRANT
- FRENETIC
- CONVOLUTED
- PLAUSIBLE
- HAIL
- ENUNCIATE
- FELICITY

The Study Partner
- MUNDANE
- ENIGMATIC
- KEEN
- SKEPTICAL
- ENCROACH
- JUDICIOUS
- INACCESSIBLE
- THERAPEUTIC
- SPORADIC
- BUTTRESS
- PLACID
- AMIABLE
- PROPENSITY
- PERNICIOUS
- CONFOUND
- DISPEL
- SUBDUE
- HARANGUE
- EARNEST
- INNOCUOUS

Rumor Chick: The Diary
- CACOPHONY
- CLAIRVOYANCE
- INCISIVE
- BENIGN
- VACILLATE
- OBSTREPEROUS
- BELITTLE
- VOLUMINOUS
- ARCHAIC
- PATRONIZE
- INCONTROVERTIBLE
- PRECARIOUS
- DISMISS
- OBSTINATE
- DISSIPATE
- CIRCUMVENT
- INDIGNATION
- PENITENT
- GENIAL
- INCORRIGIBLE

Rumor Chick: The New Guy
- ASSIDUOUS
- OMINOUS
- QUELL
- MANIFEST
- BEMUSE
- ESTRANGE
- SUPPLANT
- NOTORIOUS
- ADULATION
- ADMONISH
- CONCUR
- COMPLICITY
- POIGNANT
- CUNNING
- ASCERTAIN
- MOROSE
- REBUKE
- RECIPROCATE
- RENOUNCE
- CONCEDE

Shall We Dance? Part 1
- BANAL
- DISPOSITION
- IMPASSIONED
- ENTICE
- CONTRIVED
- EMBELLISH
- DEPRECATE
- OBTUSE
- TUMULTUOUS
- INDIFFERENT
- CONVIVIAL
- RETICENT
- VIVACIOUS
- ESOTERIC
- FACILITATE
- AFFABLE
- STAGNANT
- TRIVIAL
- PARTISAN
- COMPETENT

Shall We Dance? Part 2
- CONFORM
- PROPRIETY
- CONSTRAIN
- INNATE
- WAVER
- UNIFORM
- INSINUATE
- PERPETUAL
- CEREBRAL
- WHIMSICAL
- SQUANDER
- ADVERSITY
- PERTINENT
- AUSTERE
- ABSTRUSE
- CLANDESTINE
- CONDONE
- OFFICIOUS
- DISCREPANCY
- EMINENT

Shall We Dance? Part 3
- DISSEMBLE
- CYNICAL
- TORPOR
- EPHEMERAL
- DISCREDIT
- TACT
- PREDILECTION
- MIRTH
- INHIBIT
- DISPASSIONATE
- CORROBORATE
- INCONSEQUENTIAL
- ARTICULATE
- POLARIZE
- TENACITY
- CAUSTIC
- BOISTEROUS
- COGENT
- LATENT
- ADEPT

The Artists Part 1
- ECCENTRIC
- VENERATE
- OPAQUE
- EMULATE
- ABSTINENCE
- TRANQUIL
- AESTHETIC
- AMALGAM
- MUTABLE
- CANDID
- ACERBIC
- AUTONOMY
- BELIE
- RECLUSIVE
- NOSTALGIA
- ENTHRALL
- COLLABORATE
- GALVANIZE
- ABHOR
- INNOVATIVE

The Artists Part 2
- MEAGER
- DELINEATE
- CONCISE
- EFFICACIOUS
- ACCORD
- DUBIOUS
- LAUD
- ANTAGONISTIC
- BERATE
- AWE

Stranded! Part 1
- SERENE
- RUDIMENTARY
- EMPIRICAL
- OBLIVIOUS
- RESENT
- EFFACE
- CONSOLIDATE
- FATUOUS
- OBSOLETE
- ANIMOSITY
- REVOKE
- REFUGE
- SCOFF
- USURP
- UNDERMINE
- EXASPERATE
- FLOURISH
- RECONCILE
- EXPLOIT
- VOLATILE

Stranded! Part 2
- RAVENOUS
- ILLUSORY
- FUTILE
- IMPASSIVE
- TRITE
- SUBSTANTIATE
- LANGUID
- VERBOSE
- INCONGRUOUS
- ARDOR
- PRISTINE
- CAJOLE
- COMPEL
- DUPLICITY
- RESOLVE
- ACCLAIM
- ADROIT
- PERSEVERE
- CONCILIATE
- OPPORTUNE

Stranded! Part 3
- DESPONDENT
- BUOYANT
- COPIOUS
- INCREDULOUS
- LAMENT
- ENHANCE
- HOMOGENEOUS
- SUPPRESS
- EXPEDITE
- APPREHENSIVE
- DEBUNK
- LACONIC
- VULNERABLE
- EXTOL
- ELUCIDATE
- NEBULOUS
- EULOGY
- SOLEMN
- FEASIBLE
- EXUBERANT

Imaginary Larry

AMBIGUOUS
SCRUPULOUS
ADORN
CAMARADERIE
SPECIOUS
REFUTE
DELETERIOUS
HEED
ORTHODOX
CONSTRUE
ELATED
SCORN
TEMPER
FLORID
GARRULOUS
THWART
APPEASE
ENCOMPASS
CARNIVOROUS
ADVOCATE
NEGLIGIBLE
GRATE
BOLSTER
DISCERN
FACILE
OBTRUSIVE
INGENUOUS
DISCRETE
REPUDIATE
INVOKE

Imaginary Larry: The Fellowship of the Meyerson

VAPID
AMELIORATE
ZEALOUS
UNASSUMING
DIVISIVE
MAGNANIMOUS
TREACHERY
SPURIOUS
SCRUTINIZE
LUCID
ARID
AMICABLE
INDIGENOUS
ESPOUSE
INSULAR
LAVISH
CALLOUS
VIGILANT
CIRCUITOUS
DIGRESS

Imaginary Larry: The Battle for Desert Malaguay

AMENABLE
ORNATE
VILIFY
EXTRAVAGANT
INSTIGATE
BELLIGERENT
EVOKE
COHESIVE
ENTRENCH
PRAGMATIC
DISSENT
ALIENATE
CONSENSUS
DENOUNCE
RELINQUISH
SUBVERT
CONSTITUENT
BURGEON
PROSPERITY
HACKNEYED

Mad Scientist Part 1

DISGRUNTLED
PROLIFIC
REVERE
RESOLUTE
AUSPICIOUS
MERCURIAL
PROSAIC
SMUG
NOVEL
EBULLIENT
OBDURATE
FOSTER
EXACTING
DIMINUTIVE
ERUDITE
ANECDOTE
AUDACITY
IMPUGN
HINDER
SHREWD

Mad Scientist Part 2

INTELLIGIBLE
ALACRITY
BRUSQUE
SPURN
PUGNACIOUS
FORTHRIGHT
CONJECTURE
PERVASIVE
DEMEAN
DIFFIDENCE
CONTRITE
EFFUSIVE
TRANSITORY
DECORUM
ILLICIT
BOMBASTIC
DISCREET
ERRATIC
IMPERIOUS
DOCILE

Speedwalkers: The Legend of Max Wind

CHRONIC
DERIDE
IMPEDE
POMPOUS
CONTEMPT
BRAZEN
PERSPICACITY
JADED
SUCCINCT
MOLLIFY
INVIGORATE
DIVULGE
FRIVOLOUS
CATHARTIC
DOGGED
ENERVATE
DOUR
FLAGRANT
VICARIOUS
EUPHORIA

Speedwalkers: The Rise and Fall of René DuPont

APATHETIC
ENUMERATE
RESILIENT
EXEMPLARY
IMPETUOUS
OPULENT
WARY
COMPLACENT
IDIOSYNCRATIC
CORDIAL
CANTANKEROUS
AVARICE
DECRY
PRECIPITOUS
BENEVOLENT
DISDAIN
INSOLENT
GRATUITOUS
STEADFAST
SOMBER

Johnny Hightower Part 1

SOLICITOUS
HAMPER
ASTUTE
INSIPID
VINDICTIVE
TERSE
GRANDIOSE
EQUIVOCAL
IRATE
EUPHEMISM
INTRANSIGENT
AMBIVALENT
ARBITRARY
STOIC
DENIGRATE
ERADICATE
ACUITY
NEGLIGENT
PRUDENT
ELUSIVE

Johnny Hightower Part 2

PROPAGATE
EXORBITANT
ATROPHY
CONTEND
CIRCUMSPECT
EXACERBATE
ALLEVIATE
ALTRUISTIC
DISPARITY
VINDICATE
DEARTH
UTILITARIAN
PRETENTIOUS
PROFOUND
COMPROMISE
COHERENT
PROVOCATIVE
ANACHRONISTIC
INDICT
IMPECCABLE

Stranded! Part 4

PLIABLE
COGNIZANT
MITIGATE
PROLIFERATE
HERETICAL
GREGARIOUS
CONSCIENTIOUS
FRUGAL
ESTEEM
AMORPHOUS
PROVINCIAL
EVANESCENT
AFFLUENT
CAPRICIOUS
INHERENT
CREDIBLE
AUGMENT
PREVALENT
LUXURIOUS
INDULGE

APPENDIX C: CATEGORY LIST

Bad Blood: Words related to hatred

ABHOR	*to hate*
ACRIMONY	*hostility*
ANIMOSITY	*bitter hostility*
ANTAGONISTIC	*hostile*
CONTEMPT	*a lack of respect and intense dislike*
DISDAIN	*intense dislike*
ENMITY	*hatred*
RANCOR	*hostility*
SCORN	*intense hatred or disrespect*

BFF: Friendly words

AFFABLE	*friendly*
AMIABLE	*friendly*
AMICABLE	*friendly*
CAMARADERIE	*goodwill among friends*
CORDIAL	*friendly, warm, polite*
GENIAL	*friendly, cheerful*

Chill: Words related to peacefulness

COMPOSED	*calm*
EQUANIMITY	*calmness*
PLACID	*calm, quiet*
SERENE	*calm*
TRANQUIL	*calm*

Cocky: Words for people who think they're better than you

BOMBASTIC	*using arrogant or pretentious speech*
CONDESCEND	*to deal with people in a superior manner*
GRANDIOSE	*falsely exaggerating one's worth*
HAUGHTY	*snobbish; overly proud*
PATRONIZE	*to treat condescendingly*
POMPOUS	*exaggeratedly self-important*
PRETENTIOUS	*claiming unjust standing*

Cry Baby: Words related to sadness

DESPAIR	*a complete loss of hope*
DESPONDENT	*depressed, having no hope*
DOUR	*gloomy*
LAMENT	*to regret; to show grief for*
MELANCHOLY	*sad; gloomy*
MOROSE	*gloomy*

Eagle Eye: Words related to perceptiveness

ACUITY	*sharp perception or vision*
ASTUTE	*having sharp judgment*
DISCERN	*to detect or perceive*
INCISIVE	*penetrating, clear and sharp*
KEEN	*sharp, perceptive*
PERSPICACITY	*a high level of perception or understanding*

Feel Better: Words about making things better

ALLEVIATE	*to make more bearable*
MITIGATE	*to lessen in force or intensity*
MOLLIFY	*to soften, to ease the anger of*
TEMPER	*to soften or moderate*

Fight Club: Words related to hostility

BELLIGERENT	*eager to fight*
CANTANKEROUS	*ill-tempered*
CONTEND	*to compete; to argue*
IRATE	*enraged*
PUGNACIOUS	*eager to fight*

Flashy: Showy, decorative words

FLAMBOYANT	*highly elaborate; showy*
FLORID	*elaborately or excessively ornamented; flowery*
GARISH	*flashy, tastelessly loud and brightly colored*
ORNATE	*excessively decorated*

Gone with the Wind: Words for things that don't last long

ELUSIVE	*tending to escape*
EPHEMERAL	*lasting for a brief time*
EVANESCENT	*fading away*
EVASIVE	*tending to escape*
TRANSIENT	*existing only briefly*
TRANSITORY	*existing only briefly*

Happy Camper: Words related to happiness

BUOYANT	*cheerful*
ECSTASY	*intense joy or delight*
ELATED	*filled with delight*
EUPHORIA	*a feeling of great happiness*
FELICITY	*great happiness*
MIRTH	*gladness, amusement, laughter*
SANGUINE	*cheerful*

Hip Hip Hooray! Words related to praise

ACCLAIM	*to praise*
ADULATION	*excessive flattery*
COMMEND	*to praise*
EXALT	*to elevate, glorify, or praise*
EXTOL	*to praise*
LAUD	*to praise*

Killer: Words for harmful things

BANE	*a cause of death or ruin*
DELETERIOUS	*harmful*
PERNICIOUS	*deadly or destructive*

Like-Minded: Words related to agreement or similarity

ACCORD	*agreement*
CONCORD	*agreement*
CONCUR	*to agree*
CONFORM	*to be similar; to adapt*
CONSENSUS	*general agreement*
UNIFORM	*always the same*

Noise Pollution: Words for loud things

BOISTEROUS	*noisy; disorderly*
CACOPHONY	*jarring, disagreeable sound*
OBSTREPEROUS	*noisily and stubbornly defiant*
TUMULTUOUS	*disorderly or noisy*

Old School: Words for old things

ARCHAIC	*outdated; really old*
OBSOLETE	*no longer in use or current*

Overboard: Words for excessiveness

EXORBITANT	*excessive*
EXTRAVAGANT	*excessive*
LAVISH	*excessive; plentiful*
LUXURIOUS	*rich and superior in quality*
OPULENT	*rich and superior in quality*

Party Hearty! Words related to peppiness

EBULLIENT	*enthusiastic, lively*
EXUBERANT	*lively*
VIVACIOUS	*lively*

Pig-Headed: Words related to stubbornness

DOGGED	*stubbornly persevering*
DOGMATIC	*stubbornly and arrogantly opinionated*
INTRANSIGENT	*uncompromising*
OBDURATE	*stubbornly persistent in wrongdoing*
OBSTINATE	*stubborn*
TENACITY	*persistence, determination*

Played Out: Words describing boring things

BANAL	*ordinary and commonplace*
HACKNEYED	*overused*
INSIPID	*lacking flavor or zest; dull*
MUNDANE	*ordinary, commonplace*
PROSAIC	*lacking in imagination; dull*
TRITE	*uninteresting because of overuse*

Road Block: Words about stopping or preventing action

HAMPER	*to prevent the movement or action of*
HINDER	*to be or get in the way of*
IMPEDE	*to be or get in the way of*
INHIBIT	*to hold back; to restrain*
THWART	*to stop or prevent*

Serious Business: Serious words

EARNEST	*showing deep sincerity or seriousness*
SOLEMN	*serious and sober*
SOMBER	*gloomy*

Shady: Words for trickery

CUNNING	*clever, sneaky*
DUPLICITY	*deception, deceit*
GUILE	*skillful deceit*
TREACHERY	*deliberate betrayal of trust*

Thumbs Down: Words for disapproval

ADMONISH	*to gently criticize or warn*
BERATE	*to criticize severely or angrily*
CENSURE	*to criticize severely*
REBUKE	*to criticize or find fault with*
REPROACH	*to criticize or express disappointment*
SCATHING	*harshly critical*

Tight-Lipped: Words for being quiet and not speaking

CONCISE	*expressing much in few words*
LACONIC	*using few words (often rudely or mysteriously)*
RETICENT	*restrained or reserved*
SUCCINCT	*precise expression using few words*
TERSE	*expressing much in few words*

Trash Talk: Words for saying bad things about something

BELITTLE	*to speak of in an insulting way*
DECRY	*to condemn openly*
DENIGRATE	*to attack the reputation of*
DENOUNCE	*to condemn openly*
DEPRECATE	*to mildly insult or belittle*
DERIDE	*to speak of or treat with cruelty*
DISPARAGE	*to speak of in an insulting way*
VILIFY	*to say bad things about, to make into a villain*

Unpredictable: Words for changeable or random things

ARBITRARY	*determined by impulse or chance, without reason*
CAPRICIOUS	*impulsive, unpredictable*
ERRATIC	*irregular*
IMPETUOUS	*impulsive, unthinking*
MERCURIAL	*changeable, erratic*
MUTABLE	*subject to change*
VOLATILE	*explosive, tending to change*
WHIMSICAL	*impulsive, fanciful*

What the—? Words for unknown or uncertain things

ABSTRUSE	*difficult to understand*
AMBIGUOUS	*unclear*
AMORPHOUS	*lacking definite form*
ENIGMATIC	*puzzling*
EQUIVOCAL	*uncertain, vague, misleading*
ESOTERIC	*understood by only a few*
NEBULOUS	*hazy, vague, or confused*

Wise Guy: Words for wisdom or cautiousness

CIRCUMSPECT	*cautious and wise*
DISCREET	*careful in one's conduct or speech*
JUDICIOUS	*having good judgment, prudent*
PRUDENT	*wise; careful*
SAGACIOUS	*insightful and wise*
SHREWD	*smart in a sneaky or tricky manner*

X-treme Intensity! Words for strong feelings

ARDOR	*energy, intensity, enthusiasm*
FERVENT	*greatly emotional or enthusiastic*
GALVANIZE	*to stimulate*
IMPASSIONED	*filled with passion*
ZEALOUS	*filled with or motivated by enthusiastic devotion*

CPSIA information can be obtained at www.ICGtesting.com
Printed in the USA
BVOW020555140812

297816BV00006B/1/P

9 780615 451749